# THE MARGUERITE AND AIMÉ
# MAEGHT FOUNDATION

MAEGHT ÉDITEUR

# Foreword

A dream landscape highlighted by the South of France sun. And at the heart of this landscape, a living centre stands serene and protected from the onslaughts of the world. A "lived-in place" is the much repeated expression found in visitors' comments, even though its sole inhabitants are inanimate objects which convey an immensely powerful sense of soul. And yet, more than a quarter-century after the inauguration of the Marguerite and Aimé Maeght Foundation, which each year welcomes crowds of art-lovers and curious visitors from the four corners of the world, how can one not speak of the immense intellectual and financial efforts that, against all the odds, went into the Foundation's creation to ensure that what began as a chimera might become the reality which is today recognised as indispensable.

As I stand at the threshold of this book, my first thoughts obviously go to my parents to whom I wish to express my gratitude as, without them, the project would certainly never have seen the light of day. Given the context of the 60's, enormous courage was needed to undertake such a risk-laden adventure. In those days, the incomprehension between the world of contemporary art and the general public, you must remember, was quite widely the rule and museums were not as popular as they are today, particularly for the large, prestigious exhibitions. From this point of view, the Foundation has certainly helped change the way in which our contemporaries see the art of their time. It was as if the intelligibility of the space made the works themselves, in turn, more intelligible, giving them credibility in the eyes of a somewhat perplexed public. All the more so, as the Foundation was never intended to mirror traditional-style museums, which many people felt were unwelcoming, too rigid and too cut-off from life. The Foundation is not only a living and welcoming exhibition space, but also a place open to other arts, to interdisciplinary exchanges and encounters of all kinds bringing young creators into frequent contact with more well-known artists. A public place at the public's disposal, the Foundation is — and always has been — a home for those artists who enjoy being there or finding others there at the exhibitions which are excellent occasions for exchanging and confronting ideas. These are not empty words — they are indeed *at home*, living there for a short while or working in complete freedom in the quiet of the studios.

It is to the artists, just as importantly, that I would also like to express my gratitude. From the beginning, not only did they agree with the project of the Foundation, but they adopted it to the extent of collaborating with great enthusiasm, as we shall see, at each step of its elaboration, donating works which at first constituted and later enriched its collections. This deep commitment to a common fight for what was beautiful brought together an art dealer, artists, great poets and, later on, collectors also wishing to support the Foundation with donations — not to mention the many "Friends" prompt to join them or the many collaborators who shied away from nothing to help the project come to fruition. This is, without doubt, what movingly characterized the particular nature of the whole adventure. And then, the Foundation needed a legal status that would guarantee its autonomy and full independence. Here again, my parents took steps to make it the only museum in France to function and develop with no subsidy whatsoever.

At a time when economic considerations hold sway over all other motivations (does not contemporary patronage of the arts shield a hidden concern for profit-making?), it seemed important that I recall, without making a legend of its story, how the initiative of one man with a passion became the Marguerite and Aimé Maeght Foundation, how it lives and what its history has been.

Adrien Maeght<br>
President of the Marguerite<br>
and Aimé Maeght Foundation

# MARGUERITE AND AIMÉ MAEGHT

*"As it exists today, the project for the Foundation exceeds the wildest possible imaginings that Aimé Maeght may have had in that first moment when, having retired to Saint-Paul afflicted by a deep bereavement, he was advised by Braque, and subsequently by Léger, to undertake something that went far beyond himself."*

*Henri Maldiney, Derrière Le Miroir* n° 148
July 1964

The 28th July 1964, André Malraux, the French minister for Cultural Affairs, was handed by Marguerite and Aimé Maeght's grand-daughters, Isabelle, Florence and Yoyo, a red cushion bearing the keys to the Maeght Foundation. The Foundation was the first "museum" of modern art to be built in France since 1936 when the Musée d'Art Moderne de la Ville de Paris had been opened. In reality, it is rather less a museum than a space that welcomes all forms of contemporary art.

What was attempted here was entirely the work of one couple, Marguerite and Aimé Maeght, empassioned by living art. The architectural complex is more than a simple testimony to an art dealer's success: "What has been attempted here has never been attempted before: the instinctive and moving creation of a universe in which modern art could both find a place and come into contact with the invisible world that was formerly known as the supernatural [1]" André Malraux was to declare at the time.

Marguerite and Aimé Maeght made plans for the Foundation's walls to be raised on a sunlit hillside overlooking a ravine in the South of France. But this site would have been of little use, had it not been for the strong presence of the artists, and the collaboration of the architect, Josep Lluis Sert.

The project took a long time to mature but, in coming to life, it revealed the couple's taste and talent for creating spaces and atmospheres. Throughout their lives, Marguerite and Aimé Maeght were to invent "residences" that favoured tranquillity, confidence and a receptivity to art. The Maeght Foundation was born of this clear and confident relationship with the world. It also testifies to the exceptional history of one man and one woman.

◄ *Marguerite and Aimé Maeght at Braque's home,*
*in Varengeville, in 1952.*

9

The studio of the Ecole des Beaux-Arts de Nîmes.
Aimé Maeght's place is marked with a cross.

Aimé Maeght's C.A.P. (professional certificate),
the only degree he ever obtained and which his future was based on.

*Aimé Maeght after leaving the technical junior high school in Nîmes.*

Born on 27th April 1906 in Hazebrouck (Nord), the son of a railway company employee, Aimé Maeght spent his childhood near Nîmes in the Cevenol region of southern France, where his war-widowed mother had been repatriated by the Red Cross.

Marguerite Devaye was born on the 25th August 1909 in Cannes (Alpes-Maritimes), the youngest child in a family of local tradespeople.

Declared a ward of court, Aimé Maeght became a boarder at the Nîmes junior high school, where he showed interest in reading, drawing and music. His grandfather, whom he greatly admired, introduced Aimé to the violin, which later led to the creation of an amateur jazz orchestra, *Le Banana's King Jazz,* together with friends. As member of the orchestra, Aimé was equally at ease playing the violin, the banjo or the drums, setting the local

11

*Marguerite and Aimé Maeght*
*on their wedding day,*
*31st July 1928.*

young people's feet tapping. He finished his training at the technical high school in Nîmes and in 1925 qualified as a lithographer-draughtsman.

Shortly afterwards, he settled in Cannes and began work at the Robaudy printing works where he rapidly progressed. As a colour print operator, Aimé Maeght was responsible for reproducing the works of art. He would execute the transferrals, drawing on the back of tracing paper the outline that was to be transposed onto stone or plates. Aimé excelled at this task, revealing an innate sense of colour.

It was at this time he met the woman who was to become Marguerite Maeght. The marriage took place on 31st July 1928 and two years later, in 1930, Adrien Maeght was born. That same year, the couple set up the Imprimerie des Arts which continued to function until 1946.

In 1936, while still working for Robaudy, Aimé Maeght opened a furniture and Clarville radio shop in the Rue des Belges in Cannes. At the back of the shop, he continued his lithographic work, creating numerous

12

*Aimé Maeght and Pierre Bonnard, in Cannes, in 1943.*

logos, packaging designs and posters. It was then that he met Pierre Bonnard, who had come to Robaudy's to have a poster made for a charity gala given by Maurice Chevalier and organised by the Red Cross for the retired artists of Ris-Orangis. Bonnard was to pay homage to Aimé Maeght, appreciating both his extraordinary talent as a layout artist and his sense of colour. "One senses that you have studied chromolithography," remarked the painter "to be able to match this beige and red with the skin colour." Marguerite Maeght, for her part, hung up various paintings to decorate the walls of her shop. Paradoxically, the war turned the Riviera into the economic and financial pole of conquered France and the region fast became the centre of an effervescence hitherto unknown.

13

The shop supplies, however, dwindled away due to the lack of manufactured products. All that remained were the paintings on the walls... and they started to sell!

The shop gradually became transformed into an art gallery exhibiting works by local artists such as Pastour and Jaulme. Aimé Maeght did not stop there. He went on to encourage other artists to exhibit in his gallery: Pougny, Jean-Gabriel Domergues, Sébastien, André Marchand, Dany Lartigue... The name chosen for the gallery was Arte.

*The Arte gallery, rue des Belges, in Cannes.*

14

While Aimé was mobilised in Toulon, Marguerite Maeght contacted Pierre Bonnard who had settled near Le Cannet. He was never to forget the story of their first meeting. Marguerite, who little suspected the painter's renown, did not doubt for an instant that she would obtain a painting from the master and equally assured him that the prices he was proposing were quite unreasonable. Did she not sell Pastour's paintings? Bonnard, amused, nonetheless gave her a painting to sell without lowering his price. No sooner was it placed in the window than it was sold — to the great surprise of Aimé Maeght who had since returned from Toulon. It was this shared passion for painting which gave rise to a friendship full of long discussions on contemporary art.

In 1942, the family grew larger with the birth of a second son, Bernard. The following year, Bonnard introduced Marguerite and Aimé Maeght to Henri Matisse who was living in Vence, only a hundred metres or so from their house. In 1944, in collaboration with Jacques Kober, the Pierre à Feu publications came into being. Aimé Maeght published for them the first

*André Chastel, "Portrait of Marguerite Maeght and her sons", 1942, oil on canvas, 97 × 130 cm.*

15

*Invitation card by Henri Matisse for the inaugural exhibition of the Maeght gallery in Paris in 1945.*

works of a collection of the same name: *Provence Noire* illustrated by André Marchand, *Miroirs profonds* by Henri Matisse...

By the time of the Liberation, Aimé Maeght had already developed worthwhile professional relations and Bonnard advised him to move to Paris, accompanying him on his first exploratory visit. Luck was on Aimé Maeght's side. André Schoeller, one of the most important Paris art experts, had decided to sell his Rue de Téréhan gallery in the eighth district in Paris. Bonnard urged Aimé Maeght to buy the place, as did Matisse, who no longer had an official art dealer, by promising his most recent works for the opening exhibition.

*Alberto Giacometti, "Portrait of Aimé Maeght", 1960,* ▶
*pencil on paper, 47.5 × 31 cm.*

*Henri Matisse, "Portrait of Marguerite Maeght", 1947,* ▶
*charcoal, 61 × 47 cm.*

---

Thus it was that in October 1945, the Maeght gallery opened its doors with Matisse's most recent works. It was the beginning of intense artistic activity in all domains, bringing together painters and writers. For Aimé Maeght, books and prints were essential supports for expression and he supervised their production personally, inventing as the need arose new techniques to solve the problems posed by the artists and writers.

In 1946, came the creation of the review, *Derrière Le Miroir,* which was later to acquire a great renown. From that moment on, the small exhibition catalogues were replaced by the large-format review, originally just a single sheet of paper folded in four. The publication, illustrated with original lithographs, contained a variety of texts written by poets, writers, philosophers and critics. The Imprimerie des Arts in Cannes closed down and the typographical work was thereafter entrusted to the Imprimerie Union or to Féquet et Baudier, the lithography being transfered to the Fernand Mourlot workshop in Paris.

*Aimé Maeght and André Breton, in 1947.*

18

In July 1947, the Maeght gallery, together with André Breton and Marcel Duchamp, organised the *Seconde Exposition internationale du Surréalisme* which proved to be an unprecedented success and from then on ensured the gallery's reputation.

That same year, Aimé Maeght met Joan Miró who was then aged fifty-four. Originally from Barcelona, Miró spent his time between Paris and Spain. For the 1937 Universal Exhibition, he had painted *Le Faucheur,* an enormous mural exhibited next to Calder's *La Fontaine de mercure, La Montserrat* by Julio Gonzalez, *Guernica* by Picasso — for the Spanish Republic's pavilion, the architect of which was none other than his friend, Josep Lluis Sert. Miró entered the gallery in 1948 to join Georges Braque and Fernand Léger; Bram Van Velde, Marc Chagall, Alexander Calder and Raoul Ubac were to follow.

*Wassili Kandinsky, ''Le Nœud rouge'', 1936,*
*oil on canvas, 89 × 116 cm.*

The gallery's publishing business was becoming increasingly important with the publication of numerous book-collector's editions. Aimé and Marguerite Maeght acquired some property in Saint-Paul. In 1951, the gallery presented the works of Wassili Kandinsky and Alberto Giacometti. The gallery was, in fact, as concerned with affirming the reputation of already known artists, as with revealing young talents, such as Saül Steinberg, Pierre Tal-Coat, Pablo Palazuelo, Eduardo Chillida, Ellsworth Kelly and François Fiedler.

Aimé Maeght opened his own lithography and engraving workshops in the Paris suburb of Levallois. In 1965, these were to merge with the Imprimerie Arte at 13, Rue Daguerre in Paris, which had been created independently in 1964 by Adrien Maeght. Following on from the constellation of great masters, the gallery's 1960's exhibitions were to include works by Jean Paul Riopelle, Antoni Tàpies, Pol Bury, Valerio Adami and Paul Rebeyrolle. Yet Marguerite and Aimé Maeght were to ask nothing from all these artists save what they demanded of themselves —

*Georges Braque, "Les Oiseaux noirs", 1956-1957, oil on canvas, 129 × 180 cm.*

◀ Fernand Léger, *"La Partie de campagne" (final version), 1954,*
*oil on canvas, 301 × 245 cm.*

the ability to take risks and follow through an idea to the very end. In order to help the young artists they believed in become established, they never hesitated to sacrifice masterpieces from their own collection. They never separated the work of art from the human being who had created it. The artists were friends — once accepted, they became part of the family, to the extent that not one of them ever signed a contract.

"When there is understanding between people", as Marguerite Maeght would say, "a contract is of no use and when there is no understanding, a contract is not going to settle things [2]."

Everything was based on complete trust.

By the beginning of the 60's, the gallery had become one of the most

Adrien and Aimé Maeght with Louis-Gabriel Clayeux, in 1956.

24

*Marguerite Maeght and Marc Chagall.*

important in the world. Its godparents had been two historic figures of 20th century art: Bonnard and Matisse. The couple Aimé and Marguerite Maeght worked in total complicity, complementing each other perfectly in their choice of artists. Marguerite Maeght was to say later: "Women have greater instinct and sense danger more easily than men. I think I was useful to my husband insofar as I got him to see the other side of things, as he's always enthusiastic and a great optimist. It's not that I'm a pessimist, but I'm more logical."

Such a diverse choice of personalities — Miró, Braque, Chagall, Tal-Coat, Giacometti, Calder — was a clear sign of the gallery's refusal to limit itself to one single artistic current. With the help of Louis-Gabriel Clayeux, who was director of the gallery as of 1947, Aimé Maeght created an open space where words and images were united in an experience that had been at the origin of the whole adventure: publishing.

CATI CHAMBON

1. Foundation's inaugural speech, *Derrière le Miroir* n° 145, Maeght éditeur, Paris, 1964.
2. Conversation between Marguerite Maeght and Pierre Dumayet *Du côté de chez les Maeght* de Jean-Michel Meurice, 1973, ORTF and Maeght Productions.

Pierre Bonnard, *"Jeune fille étendue"*, 1921,
oil on canvas, 56 × 61 cm.

THE MARGUERITE AND AIMÉ MAEGHT FOUNDATION

# THE ORIGINS OF THE PROJECT

*Alberto Giacometti, Louis-Gabriel Clayeux and Josep Lluis Sert
on the terrace of the Mas Bernard, Saint-Paul.*

*"I had six hectares of land on Gardettes hill. I built my house there. But one of my sons died and I was left without a taste for anything. For the first time in my life, I began to let myself slide. I must say, the painters were once again those who suggested what course I should take. Georges Braque urged me into an undertaking that would help me overcome my grief, a place devoted to modern art right on the spot where we are, amongst the thyme and rosemary... And Fernand Léger said to me 'If you do it, I'll bring my daubings. I'll even paint the rocks'* [1]*."*

In 1953, following the death from leukaemia of Bernard, their youngest son, Marguerite and Aimé Maeght, deeply distressed, undertook a trip to the United States on the advice of Fernand Léger. During their stay, in 1955, they visited various American foundations, including the Barnes, Phillips and Guggenheim foundations. Slowly, the idea of their creating a Foundation themselves began to take shape. In a 1974 interview with the newspaper, *Le Monde*, Aimé Maeght recalled that the project had meant more to him than the mere fulfilment of a dream and that it was something secret which had been vital to him and helped him go on living. His wish was to bring together his entire collection and provide his artist friends with a place where they could work and exchange ideas. It opened up the opportunity for him to become a creator. Once again, he was ready to take risks. His Paris gallery with its one and a half thousand to two thousand paintings gave him a feeling of constraint as, in any case, he could only ever hang at most forty or fifty at a time. "I needed air and space. I didn't want to set up a super-gallery in guise of a foundation, but something that belonged to the community and, at the same time, was an independent enterprise so that it would have the power to act."

At that time, as French cultural activity was being concentrated in Paris, the choice of settling in Saint-Paul was somewhat of a challenge.

At Harvard, Aimé Maeght met the architect, Josep Lluis Serp, who had worked with Le Corbusier and, in 1931, become a member of the GATCPAC (Group of Catalan architects and technicians for the progress of Catalan architecture). The group published a journal, *Documentos de Actividad Contemporanea* (known as AC), which gave editorial support to the meridional-style architecture found in the coastal villages along the Spanish Mediterranean and typified by the architecture on the island of Ibiza. In 1955, Sert built Joan Miró's studio in Palma de Majorca and Aimé Maeght, on his first visit in 1956, was much impressed by the beauty of the site and the functional aspect of the building. At Harvard, Josep Lluis Serp and Aimé Maeght together outlined the first plans for an "ideal

29

gallery" to be built on a unique site on the French Riviera, high above the Mediterranean Sea, near the snowy peaks of the southern Alps. The drawing up of the plans was begun immediately. For three years, during which time Josep Lluis Sert replaced Walter Gropius as Faculty Director, the two men worked at making the Foundation into a place where art could be appreciated under the best conditions. Both of them were against the idea of a closed museum, a vast labyrinth where, to see a specific work of art, one has first to file past hundreds of others. Moreover, Josep Lluis Sert was all in favour of an architecture that evolved from the climate, a Mediterranean architecture made for an intense sun, a limpid atmosphere and a pleasant landscape. "Our art can respect no limits other than those which are natural, geographic, eternal. ²''

In concrete terms, the starting point for the project was a small ruined chapel dedicated to Saint Bernard, which they discovered on the Gardettes land, very close to Marguerite and Aimé Maeght's property. The couple decided to rebuild it so as to integrate it into the overall architecture of the Foundation.

From the outset, a close collaboration grew up between the architect and his "client". Scarcely a few weeks had gone by before Sert sent the first sketches to Aimé Maeght in Saint-Paul. All of the buildings, including the chapel, had been drawn, right down to the tiniest detail. The first project envisaged by Marguerite and Aimé Maeght resembled a village. It went against the monumental style in every possible way — imposing façades gave way to small volumes much like those of the houses found in villages, such as Saint-Paul. This project was finally abandoned for an even simpler one consisting of two main buildings connected by an entrance hall. The undertaking was considerable, full of unexpected happenings. The couple hesitated and then plunged headlong into the adventure.

1. *Le Monde,* 1975.
2. Speech made at the Barcelona Higher College of Architecture Student Association in 1934.

The model of the Foundation.

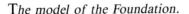

33

# KEY

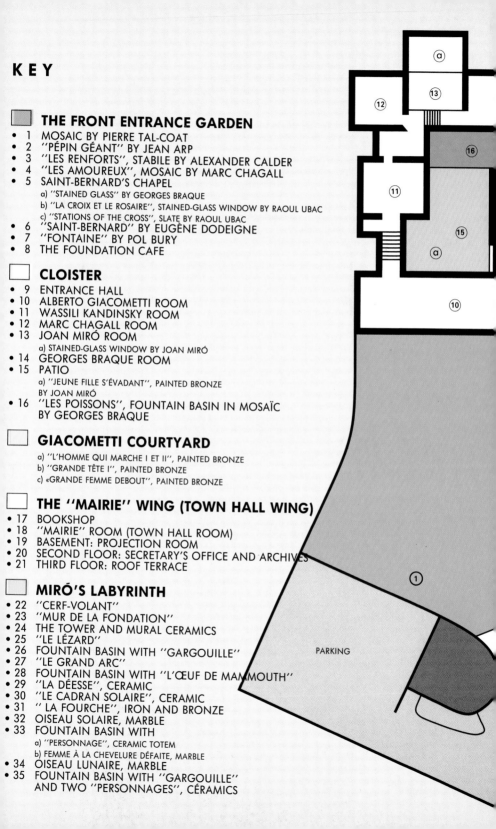

**THE FRONT ENTRANCE GARDEN**
- 1 MOSAIC BY PIERRE TAL-COAT
- 2 "PÉPIN GÉANT" BY JEAN ARP
- 3 "LES RENFORTS", STABILE BY ALEXANDER CALDER
- 4 "LES AMOUREUX", MOSAIC BY MARC CHAGALL
- 5 SAINT-BERNARD'S CHAPEL
  a) "STAINED GLASS" BY GEORGES BRAQUE
  b) "LA CROIX ET LE ROSAIRE", STAINED-GLASS WINDOW BY RAOUL UBAC
  c) "STATIONS OF THE CROSS", SLATE BY RAOUL UBAC
- 6 "SAINT-BERNARD" BY EUGÈNE DODEIGNE
- 7 "FONTAINE" BY POL BURY
- 8 THE FOUNDATION CAFE

**CLOISTER**
- 9 ENTRANCE HALL
- 10 ALBERTO GIACOMETTI ROOM
- 11 WASSILI KANDINSKY ROOM
- 12 MARC CHAGALL ROOM
- 13 JOAN MIRÓ ROOM
  a) STAINED-GLASS WINDOW BY JOAN MIRÓ
- 14 GEORGES BRAQUE ROOM
- 15 PATIO
  a) "JEUNE FILLE S'ÉVADANT", PAINTED BRONZE
  BY JOAN MIRÓ
- 16 "LES POISSONS", FOUNTAIN BASIN IN MOSAÏC
  BY GEORGES BRAQUE

**GIACOMETTI COURTYARD**
  a) "L'HOMME QUI MARCHE I ET II", PAINTED BRONZE
  b) "GRANDE TÊTE I", PAINTED BRONZE
  c) «GRANDE FEMME DEBOUT", PAINTED BRONZE

**THE "MAIRIE" WING (TOWN HALL WING)**
- 17 BOOKSHOP
- 18 "MAIRIE" ROOM (TOWN HALL ROOM)
- 19 BASEMENT: PROJECTION ROOM
- 20 SECOND FLOOR: SECRETARY'S OFFICE AND ARCHIVES
- 21 THIRD FLOOR: ROOF TERRACE

**MIRÓ'S LABYRINTH**
- 22 "CERF-VOLANT"
- 23 "MUR DE LA FONDATION"
- 24 THE TOWER AND MURAL CERAMICS
- 25 "LE LÉZARD"
- 26 FOUNTAIN BASIN WITH "GARGOUILLE"
- 27 "LE GRAND ARC"
- 28 FOUNTAIN BASIN WITH "L'ŒUF DE MAMMOUTH"
- 29 "LA DÉESSE", CERAMIC
- 30 "LE CADRAN SOLAIRE", CERAMIC
- 31 " LA FOURCHE", IRON AND BRONZE
- 32 OISEAU SOLAIRE, MARBLE
- 33 FOUNTAIN BASIN WITH
  a) "PERSONNAGE", CERAMIC TOTEM
  b) FEMME À LA CHEVELURE DÉFAITE, MARBLE
- 34 OISEAU LUNAIRE, MARBLE
- 35 FOUNTAIN BASIN WITH "GARGOUILLE"
  AND TWO "PERSONNAGES", CÉRAMICS

PARKING

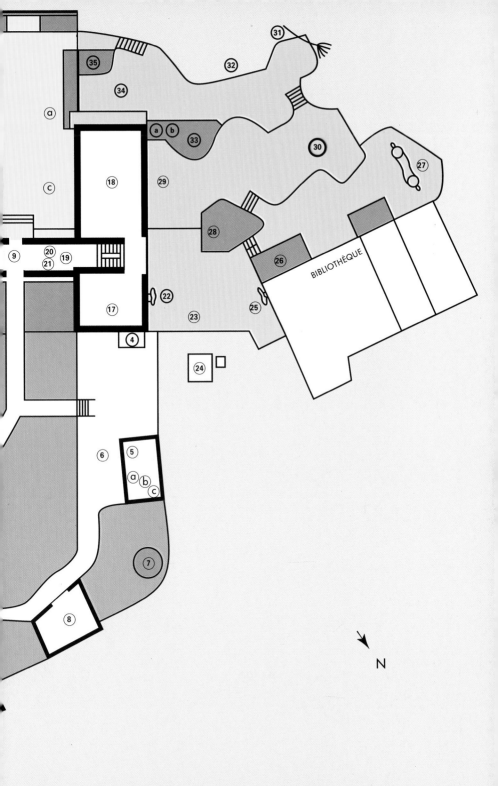

BIBLIOTHÈQUE

N

*At the "Colombe d'or", in 1962,*
*during Braque's last visit to Saint-Paul,*
*with Paule Maeght wearing a bracelet by Calder,*
*Charlie Chaplin, Jacques Prévert, Georges Braque and Mme Braque.*

# CONSTRUCTION
# OF THE FOUNDATION

Aimé Maeght, Josep Lluis Sert and Marguerite Maeght
finalising the exact position of the buildings.

38

Even before the idea came to Aimé Maeght of creating a Foundation, Saint-Paul was already a chosen spot for artists. They felt at much at home in Mas Bernard, built on Marguerite's (now nicknamed Guiguite by her friends) and Aimé Maeght's property, as at "La Colombe d'Or", the inn owned by Titine and Paul Roux.

Braque spent every January and February there, not really working, but making drawings, sketches and drafts. In the summer months, Joan Miró also stayed at the Mas with his family, giving three generations of Maeghts and Mirós the occasion to meet. Miró would take advantage of his surroundings to produce lithographs and engravings. Jean Bazaine and Raoul Ubac were also frequent visitors. Meeting there became a pleasurable habit since real affinities had grown up between the gallery's artists. And so too, writers rapidly came to join them — René Char occasionally, Paul Reverdy regularly. There, they would write the texts for the catalogues. Sartre, Paulhan and Prévert were also guests. Marguerite and Aimé Maeght's sense of hospitality was such that artists and writers felt perfectly at home in Saint-Paul.

*Joan Miró drawing on a zinc plate.*

39

For the dream to become reality, everyone was called on to take part in the Foundation's construction. Aimé Maeght was open to the most varied ideas, the only limits being technical ones. The gallery's artists were associated with the project: Georges Braque, Marc Chagall, Joan Miró, Alberto Giacometti, Alexander Calder, Eduardo Chillida, Raoul Ubac, Pierre Tal-Coat, Josep Llorens Artigas...

The first shovelful of earth was turned on 5th September 1960. The collaboration begun in Cambridge (USA), continued apace with the construction work. Bellini and Lizero, two architects from Cannes, were in charge. Each time Sert and the artists met together, new discussions arose.

*The beginnings of the construction work at the Foundation.*

40

These conversations were pursued onto the site itself, where the contours of the buildings were already becoming discernable.

At the outset, the construction work was to be carried out in three stages, staggered over ten years. Finally, the phases followed on one after the other without interruption for just under four years.

As soon as the ground was cleared and spaces had emerged, the foundations and walls began to take on the forms of Sert's Mediterranean architecture. Lunches and dinner parties were regularly prolonged by visits to the site. Priorities became clearer — the building had to be integrated into the site which, itself, had to be protected as much as possible. The plants

*The building site amidst the trees.*

and trees already there, especially the pines, rosemary and lavender, were to remain. This meant that the ideal dimensions had to be found. Everyone agreed that a huge, monumental structure would be totally out of character. The aim was not to construct a traditional museum but, yet another priority, to build a perfect gallery where works of art could be exhibited in an even, limpid, neutral and natural light. One of the main problems was the choice of light, and this called for an architectural solution. At Harvard, in January 1960, Sert and his students constructed a plywood building that could be transformed and positioned in such as way as to study how the light was distributed. The results were conclusive. Whatever the height of the sun at different times of day or in the different seasons, light rays reflected off the ground and walls fell on the paintings at an angle of forty-five degrees wihout ever dazzling the eyes of the spectator. As a result, Sert was able to perfect a special, zenithal lighting system which was used in all of the Foundation's rooms [1].

*The concrete molded impluviums topping the construction.*

The "light traps" (viewed from the exterior and from the interior).

The topography of the site was a determining factor in choosing the style and layout of the rooms, the courtyards and the terraced gardens. Their movement and changing orientation were dictated by the hillside slope and its rounded forms. Thus, the exhibition rooms, patios and gardens were laid on terraces of different levels, supported by low dry-stone walling, the overall height of the rooves remaining the same.

Originally, Sert had intended to build the surrounding and supporting walls in unsurfaced exposed concrete. However, when he saw the brickwork and stone of the region itself, he decided to change materials. He chose stone, extracted from the hillside. Brick was used between the stone and the concrete of the walls, a decision which brought the local Clausonnes brickyard back into business.

"The brick, neither light nor dark, of a pinkish brown that is tempered by the fire, is suited to the tranquillity of the courtyards. Elsewhere, used as panelling between the pillars and concrete beams, it conserves the reality of the wall by giving surface density to its elevation", as the architect explained.

It can be clearly seen that the three hundred thousand pink-sand bricks used were hand-shaped and fired in a wood-fired kiln in the local tradition. They were modelled on those of the Villa Hadriana at Tivoli, near Rome. Concrete, coated with cocoon — a film of white plaster, is used for the rest of the building, leaving the traces of the wooden planks from the original casing. The two impluviums overhanging the roof, constructed according to the principles of ancient times, lighten the construction. They collect rain water which is then channelled into the fountain basins. Aimé Maeght, only too aware of the water shortage problems common in the Mediterranean regions, liked to recall that at the origins of the Foundation lie the words of Saint John of the Cross: "The everlasting and its sound of springwater."

◀ *Aimé Maeght during the construction work*
*of the Foundation, in 1963.*

The visitor to the Foundation is struck by the coolness of the garden entrance filled with the pine-forest scents. The garden is laid out in front of the two large light-coloured brick buildings that surround the Giacometti courtyard. The terraced gardens of Miró's Labyrinth, Tal-Coat's mural mosaic and the small chapel with its Stations of the Cross by Ubac reinforce the feeling of inner peace that one experiences immediately upon entering the Foundation.

On the 28th July 1964, André Malraux was handed the keys to the Foundation by the grand-daughters of Marguerite and Aimé Maeght. At the end of the dinner, before the evening's recital given by Ella Fitzgerald and Yves Montand, the minister stood up and gave a speech to the gathered guests:

"Had we not known, Sir, what this Foundation meant to you, we would have realized it on hearing the sound of your voice for just a few minutes. It is evidently in the name of France that I share everything you have said for each and everyone, firstly for the deceased and also for the living. But, apart from the many services you have rendered to the country by your entire life — for all this is indeed the finality of a life and not some sort of accident — I should like to try to explain how this place represents for myself something quite different from a foundation and, if you will, how this evening constitutes perhaps a moment in history (...). Madam, Sir, by attempting to resume what can only be a life of love, by the very fact that the painters present are all, to some extent, either poets or else men who powerfully express the poetry of our age, you have attempted to make something which is in no way a palace, in no way a setting, and, let's say it immediately, in case the misunderstanding increase and become enhanced, which is in no way a museum. This place is no museum.

*Marguerite and Aimé Maeght,*
*on the evening of the Foundation's inauguration.*

48

◀ On the evening of the inauguration, 28th July 1964, Yoyo, Florence and Isabelle accompanied by their grandparents, Marguerite and Aimé Maeght, present the keys of the Foundation to André Malraux.

When, just a while ago, we looked at the garden area where Miró's works are situated, the same thing happened as when we looked in the room which contains Chagall's works. Those little horns which Miró reinvented with all their incredible oniric force, are now creating a relationship with nature, as in its trees, which has never been created before.

When we speak of foundations, the most famous American foundation, the Barnes foundation, were it here, would bear no resemblance with what you have created; it would seem fifty years behind, because, as admirable as it is, it is still a museum. But, here, something has been attempted which has never been attempted before: you have created the universe, created, instinctively and lovingly, the universe in which modern art could find both its place and the other world once called supernatural.

After Aimé Maeght's address, André Malraux gives ▶ his inaugural speech. Marguerite Maeght is on his left.

52

This work has barely been finished and we are silent as after the last blow of the hammer. Shakespeare comes to mind: "It is by such a night as this, Jessica..." Indeed, it is by such a night as this that silence reigned after the last hammer blow was given to the Parthenon, it is by such a night that Michael-Angelo listened to the last blows of the hammer which constructed Saint Peter's.

Madam, Sir, I raise my glass to he, who, at some future time, when, people will be bowing down murmuring and bent low, on the place where Paris once stood, having written 'here painting grew between the paving stones', to he who will come here and will say 'this relationship, which is the one we ourselves now have with life and which was born of painting, was perhaps obscurely born this night'. And, when this place no longer exists, then he to whom I raise my glass will make a brief inscription which says 'something spiritual perhaps took place here'."

On that summer night of 1964, the Maeght Foundation thus became the first space of contemporary art dedicated to living art.

1. See Chapter *Visiting the Foundation.*

*Eduardo Chillida, "Iru Burni", 1966-1969,*
*granite, 105 × 99 × 93 cm.*

58

THE MARGUERITE AND AIMÉ MAEGHT FOUNDATION

# IV

## VISITING THE FOUNDATION

# The front entrance garden

Once through the gates of the Foundation, pine trees stretch out on either side of the path leading up to the building's entrance hall. Green lawns sprawl up to the foot of the garden wall which is covered by a Pierre Tal-Coat mosaic. Created in 1964, of enormous size — 44 metres long and 2.20 metres high — it blends into the landscape, almost to the point of becoming invisible, due to the use of earth-coloured tessera. Tal-Coat often used rigid supports for his paintings, planks of wood, cigar boxes... Stone was therefore one of his favourite materials. Although the motif chosen by Tal-Coat may seem a somewhat abstract composition, this is, in fact, far from the case. Parallel to the themes he developed in painting or drawing at the same period, this work, which draws its inspiration from Prehistory, is marked with flint veins, fault lines, witches' circles... This work inspired by Nature finds its expression in an open space where the elements, neither framed nor forced to comply with a traditional perspective, are seen as phenomena surging up out of the environment, rather like the Lascaux Grotto paintings. Tal-Coat used the porosity and the roughness of the wall to create a stone painting whose supreme model was most certainly that of the Saint-Vital of Ravenna mosaic. It thus possesses that "unspeakable undulation" that Tal-Coat talked of, created by the way the thousands of tessera, each in their own fashion, according to their size, capture the light.

In front of the garden wall, in the middle of the lawn are several sculptures — on temporary display, they change according to the exhibitions — amongst which is the *Statue pour un jardin* by Ossip Zadkine, dating from 1958. Of Russian origin, Zadkine settled in Paris in 1909 and, along with Laurens and Lipchitz, was one of the most ardent promoters of Cubist statuary before concentrating his attention on the movement of the body, replacing curves with hollows. Through these contrasts of solids and voids and broken perspectives united in bronze, Zadkine emphasized the individual value of each element. Paradoxically, the sculpture gains in unity and force, as if traversed by a vertical momentum.

Nearby stands the *Pépin géant* by Jean Arp, a French poet, painter and sculptor, a collaborator of the Blaue Reiter and an eminent member of the Dada movement in Zurich. In 1917 he created his first reliefs in wood intended for wall-hanging. As early as 1931, Arp started on sculpture in

◀ Jean Arp, "Pépin géant", 1937-1966, polished bronze, 162 × 127 × 77 cm.

61

ZADKINE

◀ *"Statue pour un jardin" by Ossip Zadkine, 1958, bronze, n° 2/6, 253 × 112 × 57 cm and Pierre Tal-Coat's mosaic.*

━━━━━━━━━━━━━━━━━━━━━━━━━━━━━■━━━━━━━━━━━━━━━━━━━━━━━━━━

the round. Rejecting straight lines, his *Concrétions humaines,* lying here on bare ground, although not figurative, evoke the metamorphoses of the human body. However, the artist never sought to reproduce Nature, but rather to "produce as a plant yields fruit". Originally, the *Pépin géant* was cast in plaster by Arp himself and transposed into stone by an assistant — this copy is the property of the Musée National d'Art Moderne de Paris. Only at the instigation of the famous art dealer, Peggy Guggenheim, in 1939, were the first casts made in bronze.

Next to Arp's work, stands a spatial sculpture by Norbert Kricke, *Grosse Fliessende.* displaying thin steel tubes in the form of a parabola. Lying on bare ground and of monumental dimensions, this work succeeds in capturing spatial energy and materialising it by abandoning the mass of the central core.

View of the Foundation entrance hall
*"Les Renforts" by Alexander Calder, 1965, stabile, 630 × 500 cm.*

64

━━━━━━━━━━━━━━━━━━━━━━━━━━━━━■━━━━━━━━━━━━━━━━━━━━━━━━━━

*Alexander Calder, "Humptulips", 1965,
stabile-mobile, 250 × 110 × 90 cm.*

Opposite, deeply anchored in the ground and as black as Nobert Kricke's work is brilliant, *Les Renforts* by Alexander Calder arch over. These painted sheet-metal sculptures first appeared around 1937 and were given the name "stabiles", at the suggestion of Jean Arp and in reaction to the "mobiles". The "mobiles", earlier works, are a construction of metallic rods and sheet metal, cut out and coloured (in the form of flowers, leaves, triangles...), suspended from the ceiling. Light and airy, they conjure up the world's vivid forces, air and water, while the "stabiles", steel constuctions placed on the ground, evoke the Earth's gravity. These two principles were soon to be combined to create a variant, the "stabile-mobile", an example of which, *Humptulips,* is to be found in the Foundation's entrance hall. Although standing on one leg, its coloured metal plates sway in the wind.

Below the bookshop, there is a sculpture by the British artist, Barbara Hepworth, *Walnut* (Figure) from 1964. Like Henry Moore, she was concerned with sculptural mass, piercing it, hollowing it out. After her formative years in Italy, where she worked carving directly in stone, she moved onto an abstract, geometric form of sculpture and then, fascinated by Romanesque art, returned to using bronze and a human reference in her later years.

Not far from there stands *Iru Ari* (Three Stones), a granite sculpture dating from 1966-1969, by the Basque artist Eduardo Chillida, consisting of three stones assembled to form a cube whose volumes tangle and interlock, traversed by tunnels. This work appears to correspond to another, earlier work, in iron, *Iru Burni* (Three Irons), belonging to the Hastings Foundation in New York.

To the right of the entrance garden, after going up the steps that lead to the chapel, there is an immense mosaic by Marc Chagall on the wall of the Foundation, *Les Amoureux,* dating from 1964-1965. Chagall also painted for the Foundation, in 1964, a large canvas, *La Vie*. In fact, from 1950 onwards, he never ceased to think in terms of large formats. *La Vie* reflects the whole of his pictural universe, in which maternity, love, religion, music, the sun, and the city are all to be found. In each of his works, Chagall represents "prodigies"; a green-faced violinist, acrobats walking on their hands, a dancing girl on a tight-rope, a gigantic married couple and their naked child floating above the city, lovers rising up into the sky, carried

◄ T*he Foundation's bookshop and Chagall's mosaic
"Les Amoureux", 1964-1967.*

◀ Marc *Chagall, "La Vie", 1964, oil on canvas, 296 × 406 cm.*

Georges *Braque, "Stained-glass window", 192 × 142 cm.*

The *Saint-Bernard chapel.*

along by the miracle of love... Marc Chagall's familiarity with the extraordinary might perhaps have come from his memory of his childhood Hassidic education. He has no care for rules of composition or abrupt changes of scale. He blends the marvellous with the mundane, his sole concern being the harmony of his work with Nature: "Plant a painting in natural surroundings among trees, bushes and flowers. The painting must hold its own. It must be in tune. It must be in harmony with nature, an extension of nature. Be in harmony, as contrived and illogical as this may seem."

Continuing, we arrive near the chapel where a ceramic by Fernand Léger, dating from 1953, hangs on the wall. In front of this is Eugène Dodeigne's *Saint-Bernard*, dating from 1968. A human shape, barely outlined, the top part of the body emerges from the artist's simplified masses in an attitude of prayer and contemplation.

Inside the small chapel, along the white-washed walls is the *Stations of the Cross* by Raoul Ubac. Fourteen Stations of the Cross, based on the

Raoul Ubac, "Stations of the cross":
a) Station III, 1962, slate, 33 × 24 cm,
"Jesus falls under the weight of the cross".
b) Station VI, 1963, slate, 31.5 × 25 cm,
"A pious woman wipes the brow of Jesus Christ".

72

theme of Christ's Passion, each one portraying a moment starting from the condemnation of Christ to the laying of his body in the sepulchure — Christ's face is never visible. The *Stations of the Cross* is in slate, a rough stone composed of an infinite number of superposed layers that the artist has bevelled. The resulting cleavage assigns limits to the material beyond which it refuses to take on certain shapes. The directly-cut figure is not quite totally detached from the stone mass. It emanates from it while constantly remaining part of it. Raoul Ubac is a bas-relief sculptor. Forms are not drawn on the surface of the slate but are born of it and in it. While working on the slate, Ubac discovered its unsuspected colours, ranging from pink-grey to blue-black. Here he has arrived at sacred art, accepting a major iconographic constraint codified by a ritual thousands of years old.

"Religious art cannot be undertaken in the same way as secular art... Let's not forget that the way of the Cross is a direct call to prayer, that it is a matter of rendering something through an instantly transmissible and symbolic image, rather than through a sign which is too intimately

*c) Station X, 1963, slate, 30 × 25 cm,*
*"Jesus is stripped of his clothes".*

*d) Station XIII, 1963, slate, 30 × 25 cm,*
*"Jesus is taken from the cross and returned to his mother".*

73

linked with the artist. In my opinion, my original contribution could only lie in the execution of the work [1]."

Above the altar hangs a Spanish Christ from the 12th century, donated by the couturier Balenciaga. The chapel is lit by stained-glass windows. The first is *Oiseau* by Georges Braque dating from 1962, one of his marvellous transparent birds on a purple background evoking the Easter suffering. "For a long time, I had been preoccupied with birds and space. This motif came to me in 1929 for an illustration of Hesiod. I had painted birds in 1910, but they were always part of still lifes, while in my latest work, I have been very much haunted by space and movement [2]". With its wings spread out and yet motionless, the bird flying across the two-metre-high stained-glass window heralds the theme of the Resurrection, a fusion of the material and the spiritual, an opening onto infinity. The second stained-glass window is by Raoul Ubac, *La Croix et le Rosaire*. It is composed of three parts in red, blue and brown, recalling the bright colours of Medieval stained-glass windows.

Facing the front door of the Maeght Foundation's small chapel, hangs the spandrel of the 12th-century church of Saint-Vincent of Digne.

Further along is Pol Bury's fountain. This artist expressed his personal language through the use of mechanical constructions. His works, cylinders, cubes, steel and copper balls, columns and fountains... driven by electric motors or magnetic forces, explore the notion of movement. The first of his hydraulic fountains was constructed and perfected in 1976. The second created a sensation at the FIAC in Paris the following year. This work, dating from 1978, is composed of stainless steel articulated tubes and mobiles. A small invisible pump pushes the water up into the centre of the metallic structure. The falling water slowly fills up each tube, eventually causing them suddenly and unexpectedly to tip over and the water to fall down into the fountain basin. The tube, thus lightened, moves back up to its original position until the water fills it and tips it over again. With small clicking noises that combine with the murmur of the water, the numerous arms of the fountain move with the wind and the impetus of the liquid. There are similar sculptures at the Guggenheim Museum in New York, the Centre Culturel de la Communauté Française in Belgium, the Musée de l'Automobile in Mougins...

*Pol Bury, "Fontaine", 1978, stainless steel,* ▶
*230 × 410 × 270 cm.*

74

# Miró's Labyrinth

Josep Llorens Artigas and Joan Miró first met very early on, in 1919, at the Agrupació Courbet, founded by Artigas himself. The young artists were both from Barcelona, with only one year's difference in age between them as they were born respectively in 1892 and 1893. They met again in 1923 in Paris where Miró had just arrived. Artigas lent him his studio, in rue Blomet, a few metres from André Masson's studio. Their collaboration in ceramics started later, in 1942. The potter's exhibition of that year inspired in the painter the idea and wish to work in common. It took two years for the project to start up, due to Artigas' reticence. Miró regularly visited his friend's studio, once again back in Barcelona. Knowing nothing about the job, Miró scrupulously followed Artigas' instructions. From 1944 to 1946, their collaboration slowly took shape. Miró worked carefully and methodically, dealing with the preparatory studies and the models. The artist's strict demands were fulfilled only seven years later. In 1951, Artigas bought an old farm, "El Raco", in the village of Gallifa, north west of Barcelona. There Artigas built a larger and more suitable kiln that was christened *Nikosthène*, in homage to the 5th century B.C. Greek potter. In 1952, Miró joined Artigas and together they perfected their technique. In 1953 they were ready for enamelling, firing and baking their work. At last, on 25th February 1954, they undertook the first steps. Two hundred and thirty-four pieces of pottery satisfactorily underwent trials. An important exhibition in 1956 revealed this fertile collaboration to the Paris public.

Later, returning from a visit to Japan, a country with one of the most brilliant and ancient ceramic traditions, and as concerned as ever about perfection, Josep Llorens Artigas brought back the model of a so-called "Korean" kiln, used by Japanese potters. This kiln is inseparable from the *"Terres nouvelles"* to which the ceramic sculptures of the Foundation belong.

"Located under a lean-to outside the old house, it looked more distinctive and more suggestive than the one in the workshop inside the house. Without the tall chimney which usually topped ceramists' homes,

◀ *Joan Miró's Labyrinth: "L'Oiseau de la Tour", 1968,
wrought iron, 130 × 128 × 128 cm,
three mural plates, 1963, ceramic,
at the bottom, "Le Mur de la Fondation", 1968, ceramic,
1240 × 200 cm.*

the Korean kiln was instead endowed with a sort of belly pierced with holes. Lying under the roof which perhaps once sheltered a flock of animals, it resembled a large strange beast, most certainly a female and ready to lay clutches of eggs or to give birth to offspring with inexhaustable generosity. Its character is maternal, like that of Mother Nature or the Earth found in most primitive mythologies [3]."

None of these *"Terres nouvelles"* can be compared to artisan or decorative ceramics. They all possess a force that is comparable to that of the now buried art of the ancient Mediterranean peoples, inspired by potters from the Far East. The labyrinth sculptures are in the same vein.

*Joan Miró, "Le Lézard", 1963, ceramic, height: 270 cm.*

"Masks to life, women's and mothers' masks, representing the female principle in nature and fertile masculinity, tributes to the confusion of species and to the birth of hybrids, these great objects of enamelled clay could not find a more suitable site than among green plants, blooming

Joan Miró, *"Gargouille", 1968, ceramic, 95 × 85 × 25 cm.*

flowers, and gushing water, under the Mediterranean sun which blends and melts colours as does the ardour of the kiln [4]."

Accompanied by several bronzes, these monumental ceramics, which make up this garden, were mostly created between 1962 and 1963 in Artigas' "Korean" kiln. They were shown for the first time at the Maeght gallery in 1963. The monumental character of many of these works reflect an ambition dating precisely from those years, to the point of creating a Miró universe.

"The frame of mind in which I worked was monumental. I was thinking of possibly incorporating my work into architecture [5]."

No other project has been fulfilled as perfectly as this one. Miró, in order to work out his labyrinth in perfect detail, first placed full-sized

Joan Miró placed life-size plywood models of his sculptures on the unfinished terraces of the Labyrinth. The "Déesse" can be seen in the foreground and the "Grand Arc" in the distance.

82

plywood models of his sculptures on the unfinished terraces. He thereby wished to ensure that the chosen positions were the right ones and to check that each sculpture harmonised with the others and with the whole. "We change and we exchange with absolute freedom," he said. "Things are done, undone and redone. There are great masters who come to a place and who set down their masterpiece like someone throwing a stone into a pond, and it's all over. Personally, I work like any old guy. Sert and Artigas are old friends, it's essential."

Leaving the "Mairie" room, the first work one sees on the right is a huge ceramic wall, twelve by two metres. It was created using the 1960 ceramic at Harvard University (USA) as a model, and consists of 468 refractory slabs of the same size, joined together like tiles. This wall, erected in the open air, was prepared in Spain in Gallifa and then transported and installed at the Foundation in 1968.

"Le Grand Arc", was first executed in concrete and then shaped with a pneumatic drill by Miró, to be seen on the right at the bottom of the picture.

83

"The signs in the big ceramic wall are not particularly aggressive. There is a person with large bulging eyes, like an insect with long antennae, and eyes scattered here and there contemplate the visitor to the Labyrinth [6]."

The soft colours of this *"all-over"* composition are set off by the grey background. Miró was unaware of this at the time of its creation. The artist inscribed his work on the slabs, before the enamel spread over their surfaces by Artigas had undergone its first firing. Using a stick or some other pointed instrument, he scratched the dull layer of enamel and set about making a cursory sketch. This outline was then painted over with black enamel using a brush. Miró splashed or drew a thick line across his work. The stoneware slabs were then fired at high temperature (1250 to 1350 degrees), revealing, when removed from the kiln, the black forms and the background. Miró had only to add the colours which were fired at low temperature (900 degrees) in order to preserve their vitality. To the left, on the library wall is *Le Lézard*. "Climbing as if it was going to fly, turning

Joan Miró, *"La Déesse"*, 1963, ceramic, 157 × 115 cm,
and *"L'Œuf de mammouth"*, 1963, ceramic, 180 × 135 cm.

85

its face towards us, this face which is borne on its belly [7]." This work was named *Figure de Femme* by its creators while they were working on it. Its surface, which is also rough, bears fingerprints, those of Miró's fingers. The lizard almost looks like a human larva. Its round, searching face is like a ritual mask. In an earlier version the work was also given the title *Figure with arms up*. Whether a lizard, a woman or a face, does it not seem poised to take flight? According to José Pierre, the art critic, this

Joan Miró, *"Femme à la chevelure défaite", 1968,*
*white marble, 210 × 50 × 90 cm.*

87

lizard adopts the position of a watchman, with a look of lunar naivety about him, and watches over this oasis much more than the *Oiseau de la Tour* which is only a rooster.

Behind this ceramic mural, a tower rises up. Embedded in its walls are three ceramic slabs. The topmost is black with Miró's star sketched in blacklead on it, the one in the middle is white and bears a complex design formed partly of curves, while the one at the bottom is red with, at its centre, a sort of black cross and circle. At the top of the Tower there is a wrought-iron sculpture, the *Oiseau de la tour* dating from 1968. A small-scale, preliminary terracotta model of this sculpture also exists.

Further on, we go past a first ceramic gargoyle with big, green lips, dating from 1968, to arrive at *Le Grand Arc* of 1963. José Pierre reminds us that this work was "Researched eight times in terracotta from a whole rainbow of greys, pinks, blues and browns to be finally set in the paleness of the cement [8]."

Joan Miró, *"L'Oiseau solaire"*, 1968,
Carrara marble, 158 × 240 × 137 cm.

On the models to be seen at the Foundation, one face, repeated in different places, does not appear in the final version. *Le Grand Arc* rises up, majestically, like a door that leads nowhere. Once we have arrived at the foot of this work, we have to retrace our steps. Going down some steps, we come to a fountain basin in the middle of which is a lead-coloured egg in metallic grey, worn shiny over the years and covered with traces of black enamel. Facing it, the *Déesse* has ruled over the garden with unrivalled prestige, since 1963. This form was inspired by a terracotta of the first period.

Joan Miró, on the left, "Personnage" (totem), 1968,
ceramic and iron, 550 × 80 cm,
centre, "L'Oiseau lunaire", 1968,
Carrara marble, 300 × 260 × 120 cm.

"She is an enormous female painted in the colours of darkness and blood, potbellied and with her big tits everywhere, endowed with a strange kind of sex which is a turtle's shell sunk into the earth from which she is made [9]."

The silver tongue placed over this gaping hole turns the majestic sculpture into a goddess of fertility "mistress of the soil and of the harvest and through the oven which she opens mistress of the pots [10]."

At the foot of *La Fourche*, cast in bronze and iron (1963) — Miró always leaves it up to us to guess at the object that his sculpture is based on — is the *Cadran solaire* (1973), worked in ceramic. Over to the right is the second fountain basin, in which is reflected a sculpture standing on a pebble-like plinth, *Femme à la chevelure défaite* (1968). The white elongated marble is chiselled with curvilinear lines and holes. Fixed to the brick wall, the *Personnage* (1968), with its brown ceramic face, perched on a high iron support, a figure without body or arms, overhangs the

*The last fountain basin with "Gargouille" from 1964,*
*ceramic, 90 × 40 × 50 cm,*
*and "Personnage", ceramic, 1968, 90 × 30 cm.*

90

labyrinth, like an impenetrable sphinx. Facing it, there are two Carrara marbles, the *Oiseau solaire* and the *Oiseau lunaire* (1968), originally cast in bronze and then transposed in marble. Both are of imposing size. The *Oiseau lunaire* can be recognised by the arch which it has for feet. Its short wings are turned towards the sky and it has an enormous horned head. No other bird gives a greater feeling of the force of gravity. The *Oiseau solaire*, placed on a stone plinth, oscillates between the form of a sea mammal and that of a migratory bird. But it matters little, they are part of an extraordinary universe in which their strange mutations astonish no-one.

The last basin contains three fountains of which only one — formed of mechanical parts — spouts water. It is fixed onto the stone wall, next to two ancient theatre masks in ceramic, one green with the head of a reptile, the other blue with the round head of an owl. Going down a few steps we arrive in the Giacometti courtyard.

## The Giacometti Courtyard

The tension between the three façades of the building and the vast space to be seen on the south side correspond with the viewpoint that Giacometti's statues call for: the works shown here belong to the fifties, that is, to the period of Giacometti's life when he was convinced of the soundness of what he aimed at in his work and was definitely unsure of being able to fulfil that vision. Even though Giacometti was an internationally recognised artist at the time of the Foundation's creation, the fact that this courtyard exists is proof of Aimé Maeght's early interest in his work. It was in his gallery, in 1951, that Giacometti was again able to hold a solo exhibition after the war. As early as 1947, Aimé Maeght had bought sculptures from him (*L'Homme au doigt, Le Nez, Tête sur tige*). The large number of works owned by the Foundation — 35 sculptures and 30 drawings — demonstrates this sustained interest.

From this large collection, a few works, representing a single project, constitute the heart of what is exhibited in the courtyard. In 1958, the Chase Manhattan Bank commissioned Giacometti to do a monumental version of *Trois Hommes qui marchent* (1948), to be placed in the square in front of its building. Giacometti produced three ten-centimetre-high figures: a head, a woman standing and a walking man. He intended that the *Homme qui marche* should be life-size, while the *Tête* and the *Femme* were to be of larger-than-life dimensions.

91

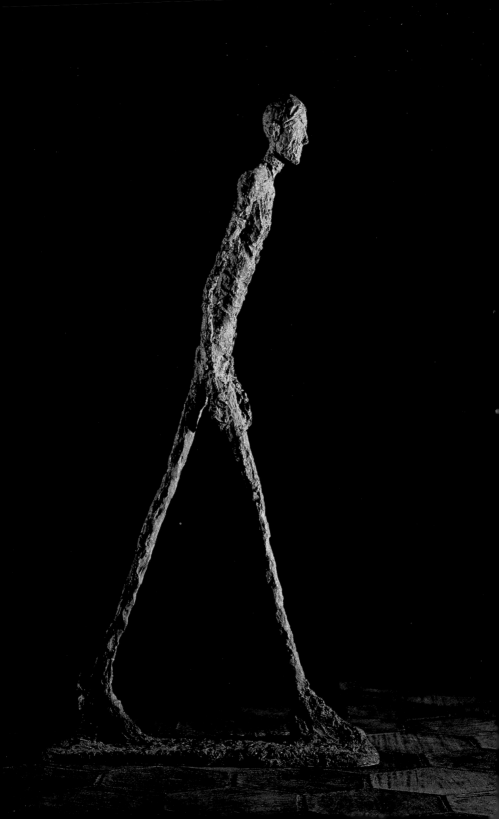

This commissioned project was finally abandoned, in part because of Giacometti's lack of zeal, but the statues were to be completed and even exhibited together at the Venice Biennale in 1962. The history of this project shows both the original closeness of the works — for the occasion specially covered with an ochre patina by Giacometti — and their refusal to become the elements of a whole. The strong presence felt in this courtyard is perhaps the awareness of this tension.

The walking man is an important theme in sculpture. For a long time, Giacometti had been interested in Rodin's interpretation of it. This theme was already to be found in Eygptian statuary, where it was used to distinguish the male from the motionless female figures. Strangely enough, Giacometti rediscovered this division when he stated: ''I have realized that I can only represent women as motionless and men walking.'' Giacometti's *L'Homme qui marche* links the horizontality of the plinth with a vertical dimension that is emphasized by the effect of the walker's thinness. Where they join, the two compact masses are as much earth as they are the man's feet. Giacometti was here seeking to grasp the unity of the ground and the man. One does not feel the weight of a man bearing down on an earth that would offer the resistance necessary for movement. Giacometti here expresses what had struck him in 1945, on the Boulevard Montparnasse: ''A man walking in the street weighs nothing, in any case, a lot less than he would if he had fainted. He balances on his legs. You don't feel his weight.'' The scientific representation of a walking person's movement — the force of gravity versus the force of cohesion — seems decidedly uninteresting in comparison. Strangely, the *Grandes Femmes Debout* are not in opposition to *L'Homme qui marche* as immobility is to movement. Here again the compact mass where the figure joins the plinth gives the impression that the figure is emerging from the earth. It stands literally facing us, and that is why Giacometti, in the title, underlined the importance of the ''standing'' posture. These women, 270 centimetres high, belong to a series of four, which constitutes the last series that Giacometti dedicated to the female nude. These figures are the tallest he ever made and are astonishing when they are put next to those created fifteen years later which, as Giacometti put it, could fit into a matchbox. And yet, in neither case was the work done on a predetermined scale. There was no attempt to miniaturise or monumentalise. It was the vision that Giacometti sought to express which imposed, to his own surprise, the work's dimensions.

In his other compositions where he assembled statues — *La Place,*

◀ *Alberto Giacometti, ''L'Homme qui marche I'', 1960, bronze, 182.5 × 26.5 × 96.5 cm, situated in the Giacometti Courtyard.*

93

◀ Aimé Maeght and Diego Giacometti, in front of "Grande Tête I" by Alberto Giacometti, 1960, bronze, 94.5 × 30.1 × 36.5 cm.

La Forêt — Giacometti had already placed a head next to standing figures. The *Grande Tête I*, the model for which was Diego, the artist's brother, also drew its inspiration from the head of the Emperor Constantine in the Capitol Museum in Rome, which Giacometti had copied one year earlier. The peculiar presence of this head within this group can be explained by the fact that it also represents a movement. The head is supported by three tiers and the figure which is focused on, appears imperceptibly through these levels without it being certain whether it is still the plinth or already the body, the throat or the neck. This emergence of the body seized in the emergence of the gaze was to be later resumed by Giacometti until his admirable and ultimate bust of Élie Lotar.

Summer 1964, grouped together on the steps of the Giacometti Courtyard, from left to right and from the top:
Jacques Dupin, Aimé Maeght, Alberto Giacometti,
Marguerite Maeght, Violette Artigas, Louis-Gabriel Clayeux,
Eduardo Chillida, Pilar Miró, Marguerite Benhoura, Adrien Maeght,
Joan Miró, Christine Dupin, Pablo Palazuelo, Daniel Lelong,
Muncha Sert, Josep Lluis Sert, Josep Llorens Artigas, Pili Chillida,
Xavière Tal-Coat, Pierrette Tal-Coat et Pierre Tal-Coat.

95

# The Interior

The option adopted by Josep Lluis Sert in the Foundation's building plan, was both simple — he copied the centripetal organisation of a Mediterranean house, closed on the outside and open around a central patio — and cleverly designed. On the garden side, the rectangular glass entrance hall, preceded by two fountain basins with sculptures in their raised centres, is closed by a screen wall, thereby gently marking off the passage from the outside to the inside. The bronze doorhandles were created by Diego Giacometti.

On the left of the entrance hall are the exhibition rooms laid out around a patio, in the middle of which is Miró's *Jeune Fille s'évadant* (1968) — the objects this work was based on can be easily identified: a tap, the lower part of a plastic dummy, united in painted bronze — and Braque's fountain basin in mosaic, *Les Poissons* (1962).

*The entrance hall of the Foundation which opens onto the patio, in the background.*

THE MARGUERITE AND AIMÉ MAEGHT FOUNDATION

Joan Miró, *"Jeune fille s'évadant"*, 1968,
*painted bronze, 135 × 60 × 40 cm.*

*The George Braque room during the Miró exhibition of 1984.*

———————————————————————————————————————■———————————————————————————————————————

The windowless rooms with their whitewashed walls and rustic floors are intersected by openings at strategic points, creating an intimate relationship between the exterior and the interior, while being at the same time relaxing for the visitor. These openings overlook the sea, the woods, the patio and Braque's basin. There are five rooms in this wing, each one dedicated to an artist and bearing his name: the Alberto Giacometti, Wassili Kandinsky, Marc Chagall, Joan Miró and Georges Braque rooms. Each one is different in size and ceiling height. The windowless walls which free up a maximum of space, enable the paintings to be hung in perfect conditions; with the light coming from the roof. This result has been obtained by the structure and the layout of the glazed semi-vaults covering the roof, which, through their various positions, capture and diffuse the sunlight into the interior. The cocoon covering the roofs increases the effect. The zenithal fanlights differ in each room, thus creating a particular light for each one of them.

Constant temperatures and humidity levels are ensured, for the most part, by the structure itself — Sert constructed double, solid-brick walls, separated by an empty space of equal thickness. To preserve the works, the temperature is maintained at nineteen degrees, except in summer when

98

it is kept at seven degrees below the ambient temperature so as not to create too great a contrast with the exterior. The humidity level is maintained at between forty-five and fifty-five hygrometric degrees.

Returning to the entrance hall, through the different rooms separated by small interior stairways, the Giacometti courtyard is on the left and, opposite, there is another wing of the building, on three levels. In the basement, is located the arts cinema which is open every day in Summer and three days a week for the rest of the year. On the first floor, there is the art bookshop which sells the Foundation's catalogues, as well as original prints, posters and postcards. Opposite the bookshop, there is the last exhibition room: the vast "Mairie" room, so-called because of its more classical design; it can also be used as a conference room. Half a floor up, is the entrance to Miró's Labyrinth. On the second floor are the secretary's office and the headquarters of the Friends of the Foundation Society. On the third floor, there is the roof terrace.

*"Les Poissons", fountain basin in mosaic by Georges Braque, 1962.*

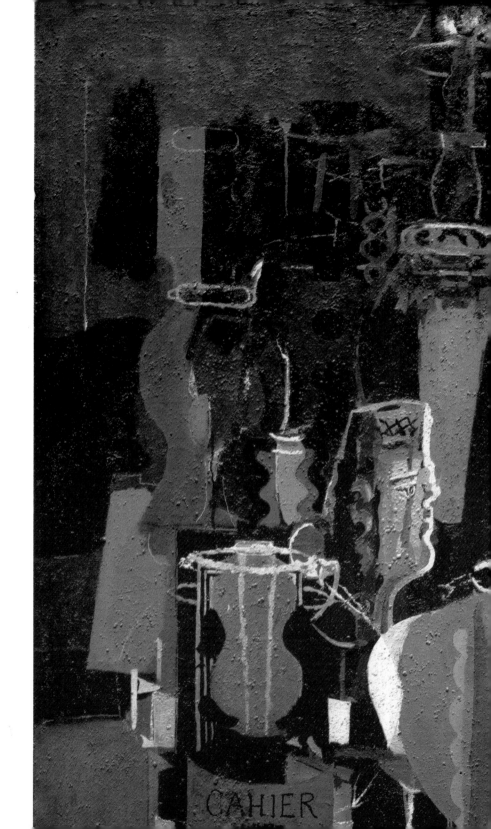
CAHIER

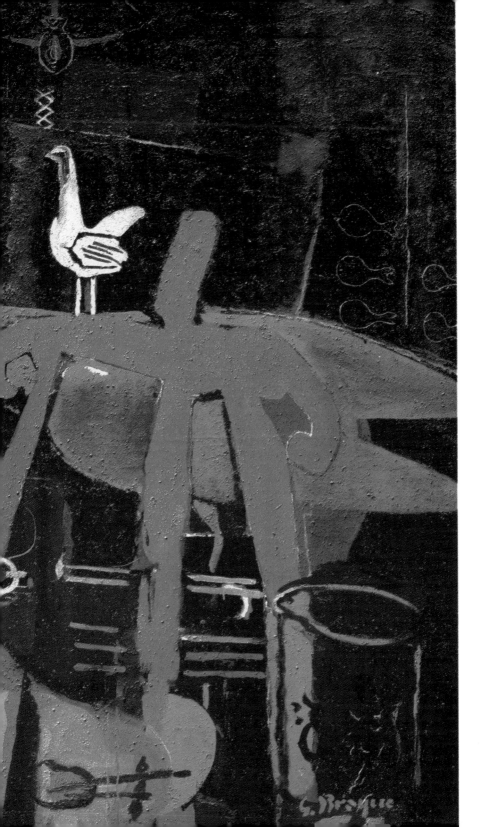

◄ *Georges Braque, "Atelier VI", 1950-1951,*
*oil on canvas, 130 × 162.5 cm.*

In 1962, Aimé and Marguerite Maeght asked Josep Lluis Sert to build a house called the House of the Artists or of the Director. The Foundation's library was then installed there, near Miró's Labyrinth. Open to the public, its collection, including 16,000 works on contemporary art (of which 15,000 in their original editions), has been built up from Aimé and Adrien Maeght's joint donation, the private library of Aimé and Marguerite Maeght and works bought by the Friends' Society. Adrien Maeght continues this work by donating to the library, as they appear, a copy of the engravings and collector's editions he publishes. It thus represents one of the best private collections of contemporary collector's editions, with books illustrated with original lithographs and etchings of limited editions, numbered and signed. These are often annotated and bear a written dedication by their authors. It is also possible to consult the main art magazines as well as the catalogues from the most important museums from all over the world, with which the Foundation has privileged contact.

The *"Mairie" room (Town Hall room).*

THE MARGUERITE AND AIMÉ MAEGHT FOUNDATION

The Foundation's café.
The chairs, stools, tables and lamps
are by Diego Giacometti.

The Foundation's café is to be found in the garden, near the entrance. Its chairs, tables, stools and lamps were created in bronze by Diego Giacometti.

1. Raoul Ubac, Collection Monographies, Maeght éditeur, Paris, 1970.
2. Jean Leymarie, L'Oiseau et son nid, in Quadrum, volume V, 1958.
3. André-Pierre de Mandiargues, Derrière Le Miroir n° 139/140, Paris, 1963.
4. André-Pierre de Mandiargues, Derrière Le Miroir n° 139/140, Paris, 1963.
5. Rosamond Bernier, "Miró céramiste" in L'Œil, n° 17, mai 1956, Paris.
6. José Corredor-Mattheos, Miró et Artigas céramiques, Maeght éditeur, Paris, 1973.
7. José Corredor-Mattheos, Miró et Artigas céramiques, Maeght éditeur, Paris, 1973.
8. José Pierre, Miró et Artigas céramiques, Maeght éditeur, Paris, 1973.
9. André-Pierre de Mandiargues, Derrière Le Miroir n° 139/140, Paris, 1963.
10. José Pierre, Miró et Artigas céramiques, Maeght éditeur, Paris, 1973.

Bram Van Velde, "Composition", 1959-1960,
oil on canvas, 130 × 192 cm.

THE MARGUERITE AND AIMÉ MAEGHT FOUNDATION

# THE FOUNDATION'S EXHIBITIONS

André Malraux and Aimé Maeght,
during the exhibition of the "Musée imaginaire".

Every year the Foundation organises several international exhibitions which represent a wide panorama of contemporary art. These may be either retrospectives of a major artist or devoted to a writer and his relationship with art. In the beginning, the Foundation mainly organised exhibitions of those artists that Aimé Maeght championed, quite simply because they played a decisive role at that time. Later on, exhibitions of other artists became increasingly important, as can be seen from the list at the end of this chapter. The hangings changed according to the exhibition and the season. In winter and spring, exhibitions presented very recent works, while the summer events were given over to artists or movements that occupy a fundamental place in late 19th or 20th-century history of art. The Foundation very often lends out works from its large collection and can, in return, borrow works from a large number of museums, galleries, collections or artists' studios.

Some exhibitions have left a particularly strong impression on all those who took part in their organisation or who visited them.

One such exhibition was the *Musée imaginaire d'André Malraux*. André Malraux's name is associated with the Foundation, since it was he who inaugurated it. He does, however, have even closer ties with the Foundation due to the opportunity offered to him in summer 1973 to transform the Foundation into his *Musée imaginaire*, which he had only been able to present in written form since 1947. The exhibition's 100,000 visitors discovered over 800 works, presenting a vast panorama of art spanning a period of four thousand years from the five continents. The selection of the works of art had been made on a principle which Malraux formulated in the words: "I only want masterpieces."

Nevertheless, the exhibition was a lot more than a simple manifestation of André Malraux's erudition and eclecticism. It was a demonstration of certain constant preoccupations. According to Malraux, our era — and its art bears witness to this — can no longer be thought of according to the same principles as previous eras. It is characterised by two particular traits: it seeks to encompass the whole world, in space and time, and yet remains unaware of its own underlying values. Modern Man — the artist included — feels compelled to know about his environment and past history, but he is unable to recognise what is at the heart of his own existence. It is this duality that animated the *Musée imaginaire* exhibition. Through this exhibition, Malraux belonged to his era, sharing its concern about future evolutions and recapitulations. Through it, he also sought to discover fundamental principles, which are present yet unperceived, and which he called the Treasure of the *Musée imaginaire*.

As early as the Foundation's inaugural speech in 1964, Malraux had stated:

"Today we know what our painting is, but we do not know what the world behind it is like. It is certainly no longer the supernatural world of crypts and religion, it is definitely not luxury."

The exhibition was something of an endeavour: would the works it brought together, while conforming to what the era called for, still reveal something about the era itself? Malraux also insisted that one should not be content just to perceive the formal relationships existing between the works exhibited.

"It is becoming clear that the *Musée imaginaire* will involve more than

*"Double Protomé", Talish, second millenium B.C.*
*Height: 8 cm*

simply demonstrating the relationships between its different forms... Visitors to the exhibition at the Maeght Foundation are going to find themselves confronted with the encounters and choices of a man born at the beginning of the century. I believe that, whether they like it or not, everyone will discover their own Treasure in the exhibition... I believe that they will sense the presence of some unknown value which has, in fact, given rise to this Treasure... I finally believe that the same is true of the whole *Musée imaginaire*: it creates its Treasure, we have only to discover it. For this reason, I cannot conceive of this museum as some grandiose, crazy adventure... And it will perhaps reveal to future generations the values which unite these works... For we are as unaware of them as we are of the other values which animate our civilisation. As it is the first to see itself as the heir to the earth's past, it is also the first to have no awareness of its own supreme values, those same values which neither you nor I confuse with the values it uses so badly as a reference [1]."

The exhibition itself was twofold: it included 633 pieces — photographs, manuscripts, books and letters — connected with Malraux's biography and 178 works of art. Amongst these, particular importance was accorded to the Middle and Far East. There were 70 pieces from Babylonia, Egypt, Afghanistan, Pakistan, India, Tibet, the Khmers, China and Japan. These included a 12th-century Japanese painting, *Taira no Shigemori* by Takanobu, a painting which is so fragile that the Jingaji temple in Kyoto exhibits it only twelve days of the year, a Hittite *Maternité*, an Oriental *Double Protomé, La Déesse de la fertilité* from the Museum of Damascus, dating from the 20th century B.C. that had never before been out of Syria, and the famous intendant *Ebih-il* by Mari. Art from Oceania was represented by 10 pieces from the Marquesas Islands, New Guinea, the New Hebrides and Easter Island. Pre-Columbian (10 pieces) and African art (13 pieces) also appeared in the exhibition. Apart from prehistoric works, Gallic remains and Greek and Medieval statues, it featured European painting, in particular: Titian, El Greco, Poussin, Rubens, Georges de la Tour, Velasquez, Chardin, Fragonard, Delacroix, Goya, Corot, Van Gogh, Braque, Picasso, Masson, Kandinsky, Chagall, Rouault, Fautrier, Miró and Dubuffet. All these artists inspired texts by Malraux. Some of them even owed him a large part of their public renown.

In the summer of 1975, with the exhibition *Bonnard dans sa lumière*, the Foundation paid homage to the painter Matisse called "the greatest of all". Even though it included some of the 600 canvases of the master who had died in 1947, which had been sequestered for probate reasons and which had never been shown to the public, the exhibition was not simply

109

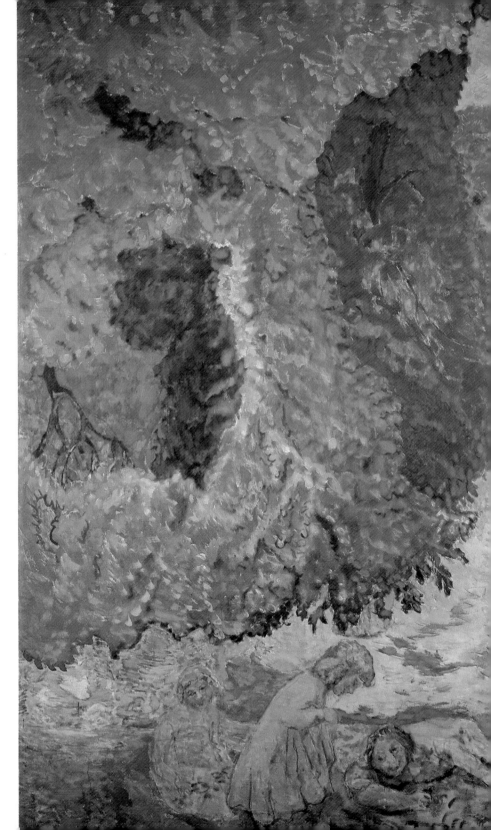

■

a retrospective of his work. It was a sincere homage by Aimé Maeght to the person who had introduced him into the art world. The friendship between the two men had been deep. Bonnard, speaking to Thadée Natanson on the subject, had confided: "Were I to have had a son, I should have wanted him to be just like that."

Indeed, Aimé Maeght had been particularly lucky in meeting at the same time, in Cannes during the war, two geniuses of the literary world who also happened to be two of the greatest painters of the time: Matisse — who inaugurated the Maeght gallery in Paris in 1947 and to whom the Foundation devoted an entire exhibition in 1969 — and Bonnard.

"Today, while painters are quite losing sight of painting, it was perhaps time that a second exhibition be devoted to Bonnard, the purest and truest of modern painters", Aimé Maeght declared at the time. His first exhibition was in December 1946, *Le Noir est une couleur,* which gave rise to the first issue of *Derrière le Miroir* and in which Matisse, Braque, Rouault and others also participated.

Aimé Maeght's career is inseparable from Bonnard's and that is why this retrospective had such special importance. The exhibition's title came from something Bonnard himself had said, six months before his death, as recounted by Jean Leymarie: "On the eve of my departure, in August 1946, Bonnard came to Cannes. We walked in silence along the edge of the bay and when he was about to leave me, as the sun was setting in all its glory behind the Esterel, and as the sea gave its evening shudder, he cried out: "Never has the light been so beautiful." He was nearly eighty years old and it was as if he were seeing, for the first time, the Cannes light that was so familiar to him. Included in the exhibition were very early canvases, such as *Femme à la robe à pois blancs* dating from 1891 and *Le Nu couché* dating from 1898. At the time, Bonnard was exhibiting at the Salon des Indépendants and formed a group, the Nabis — God's prophets — with Vuillard, Maurice Denis, Valloton, Maillol, Sérusier and Ranson. His first solo exhibition took place in 1896 at the Durand-Ruel Gallery. "Nobody renders more resolutely", Gustave Geoffroy related in his chronicle, "the appearance of the street, the fleeting silhouettes, the patches of colour seen through the Paris fog, the fragile grace of a little girl". His friends had nicknamed him the "Nabi très japonard" (very Jap-like Nabi),

112

because of his predilection for certain decorative motifs, his bird's eye views and his unexpected perspectives. Also included were paintings that had never before been seen in France, such as *Le Train et les Chalands* from 1909 and *Le Matin de Paris, Le Soir de Paris* from 1911 which showed his commitment to colourful painting. The huge work, *L'Été*, donated to the Foundation by Marguerite and Aimé Maeght, was exhibited; a symbol of the shock that Manguin — a friend of Matisse and Marquet — experienced in Saint-Tropez upon encountering the Midi: "I was stunned, like in the Thousand and One Nights. The sea, the yellow walls, the reflections as colourful as the light."

The first paintings of nudes washing also date from this period. Bonnard favours the effects of the light on his bathers' bodies, the sparkling edge of the bathtub, the reflection on a ceramic tile. The composition of his canvases *Nu à la lampe* (1910) and, later, *Nu à la baignoire* (1931), *Nu au miroir* (1931) and *Nu accroupi* (1941) is not unlike that of the *Nymphéas* by Monet — whose neighbour he had been. Just as Monet, at Giverny, had one day ceased to view his garden in a classical perspective — as if,

*Michel Guy, French Minister of Cultural Affairs, and Aimé Maeght, at the exhibition "Bonnard dans sa lumière", in 1975.*

■

leaning on the rail of the little Japanese bridge, he had hung his head over the water and seen the *Nymphéas* from this upside-down position, so Bonnard left aside the traditional perspectives of painting. Moreover, when painting, he stretched out large pieces of canvas — much larger than the final painting — on his studio walls, only cutting them down to size when the painting was finished. " ...Bonnard's iridescent nudes, left to their vegetal oblivion, sometimes open out and float like water lilies. They are utterly foreign to neo-classical standards, destructive of beauty, and refer back, beyond Venice, to Hellenistic sources [2]."

Thus Bonnard succeeds in blurring the light, in nuancing the warm and cool tones and in weaving internally — in a complex framework — a construction inherent to the painting. He organises his compositions according to different perspectives, in an afocal and centrifugal way, as for example, in *Paysage au Cannet* (1928), *Les Toits rouges* (1941) or *Portrait de l'artiste*, (1945), shown at the exhibition. What is miraculous about his painting, whether it be a landscape, an interior or a self-portrait, is that he succeeded in producing a painting which was "a series of patches which are linked together and which finish by forming the subject, the piece over which the eye wanders unhindered."

The 83 paintings, some from the Phillips collection in Washington, the Guggenheim Museum in New York, the Hermitage Museum in Saint Petersburg or the former Swiss Hahnloser collection, 62 drawings, and illustrated books, bore witness to this success.

In 1978, there was a retrospective of Alberto Giacometti's work. The Foundation, which has one of the two largest collections of this artist's work, was the predestined place for such an exhibition. One hundred and sixteen sculptures were presented, amongst them, the earliest Cubist and Surrealist works, but also the *Quatre Femmes sur socle* (1950), the *Femmes de Venise* (1956), *Diego au chandail* (1954), ten or so previously unshown plaster casts, 68 paintings including the portraits *Marguerite Maeght* (1961), *Annette* (1960) and *Yanaihara* (1960), 120 drawings and a selection of etchings, lithographs and illustrated books, a total of more than three hundred works.

115

Julio Gonzales, "Standing figure", 1932-1935, iron, 128 × 60 × 40 cm.

THE MARGUERITE AND AIMÉ MAEGHT FOUNDATION

Another major exhibition was *La Sculpture du XX<sup>e</sup> siècle, 1900-1945* — *Traditions et ruptures,* which was held in 1981, from June to October. This exhibition was the last to be inaugurated by Aimé Maeght and it took as the starting point of modern sculpture the work of Auguste Rodin (1840 - 1917). His career began with two scandals and culminated in an affair: first, the refusal of the Salon, in 1860, to exhibit the *Masque de l'homme au nez cassé* — a terracotta, which originally had split in two, then, in January 1877, the newspaper *L'Étoile belge's* accusation of duplication concerning *L'Age d'airain,* and, finally, the outcry caused by the commemorative monument to Balzac commissioned by the Société des Gens de Lettres. In fact, Rodin produced a plaster cast looking as if it had been mutilated: Balzac in an alb, giving the sensation of mass which is on the point of moving.

The exhibition then showed around 1900, parallel to Rodin's immediate posterity, the progressive development of an archaism in technique that referred back to Greek archaism. Bourdelle introduced, as is shown in the *Pénélope* of 1909, also in the exhibition, a different model to that of Rodin, with a thickset appearance resembling Greek sculpture of the 4th century B.C., with its rigid and symmetrical drapes masking the body.

The works of Maillol exhibited, *Ile de France* (1925) and *Marie* (1931), marked the beginning of a kind of sculpture which drew its strength from two antagonistic currents — one of which was crystallised in Rodin's work and the other in the Primitivist question. Maillol favoured the effects of volume and construction, carving the wood directly with no attempt at skilfulness, playing on the connections between the brutality of the material, the rusticity of the execution and the Gauguin-like motif.

Artists like Picasso first came into contact with Gauguin's sculpture at Vollard's and at the Salon d'automne of 1906. The distinction between Gauguin's work, on the one hand, and Rodin's and Cézanne's, on the other — primitive flatness as opposed to Rodin's construction and Cézanne's touch — influenced Matisse, Picasso and Derain. Although one can discern classical forms in Matisse's early works, (*Le Serf* 1900-1903) and those of Picasso (*Le Fou,* 1905), in their later works, one can see an interest in direct cutting and possibly even the transition from bronze to wood. Matisse produced the four *Nus,* two of which, *Nu II* (1913) and *Nu IV* (1930) were exhibited. Picasso preferred a geometric and synthetic art, evolving progressively towards an African primitivism which Gauguin, the initiator of this exoticism, did not possess. Brancusi's work sums up this history of primitivism. Deaf to Rodin's teachings, he moved towards stone sculpture with simplified volumes. His oval heads, *La Princesse X* (1916), 119

*Mademoiselle Pogany III* (1933), halfway between a portrait and a fetish, have a formal relationship with African sculpture and with that of Gauguin. Brancusi passes from the anatomical to the allusive. His primitivism is akin to the primordial. The artist regresses to an essential shape (the egg) and returns to the first age of art.

From 1912 to 1913, all of Picasso's artistic research was concentrated on painting, drawing and *papiers collés*. Nevertheless, he was the only one at the end of pictural Cubism to revive a kind of sculptural Cubism that was totally unrelated to his previous sculpture. He developed three-dimensional *papier collé* to arrive at collage constructed in space. *Le Verre d'absinthe* (1914), of which several versions exist, marks the predatory character of a Picasso who recuperated and metamorphosed — polychromy is inherent in this mixing and matching — simple objects. Picasso paid great attention to the physical and realistic character of the object to the point of transgressing it. Gargallo and Gonzalès used Cubist ideas to execute sculptures in metal constructed of twisted copper shavings in counter-relief. Gonzalès also perfected his soldered-iron assembled sculptures with a welder.

A radical turning-point in history came with Marcel Duchamp's *ready-mades (Roue de bicyclette,* 1913, *Porte-Bouteille,* 1914) where the object becomes a decisive frame of reference for the sculpture which loses its sacred aura.

Later, mechanisation appeared. Applying his theory of plastic dynamism, Boccioni advocated the use of all sorts of materials: wood, paper, glass and metal.

The Foundation featured importantly such artists as Gabo, Pevsner, Tatlin, Moholy-Nagy, Kobro, Steinberg and Rodtchenko who used the most modern materials of the time (plastic, iron, steel and glass) in spatial constructions of a geometric nature. Sculpture became lighter and transparency appeared, as did movement in the *Hängende Konstruktion* by Rodtchenko and in Gabo's *Construction linéaire.* The use of these new materials produced another radical change in a tradition that had existed since earliest Antiquity, just as, in a different way, Surrealism had changed works originating in the imaginary and the subconscious. Miró, Ernst and Giacometti all participated in this key movement of the twenties.

◀ *Alexander Calder, "L'Haltérophile", 1930-1944,*
*bronze, height: 21 cm.*

Calder reintroduced movement into sculpture. "Calder's art is the sublimation of a tree in the wind", wrote Duchamp who would give the name *mobiles* to his constructions that moved in the air.

Arp used strange and symbolic figures, cutting out his first reliefs in wood and then executing in plaster what he called *Concrétions humaines,* sculptures in the round placed on the ground *(Le Torse* 1931, *Pépin géant* 1937).

"However, Matisse, Laurens, Lipchitz, Marini, Zadkine, Picasso, reverted to a certain tradition. Bronze sculpture was reinstated and artists' works heralded a new trend, a new equilibrium which would not fully come into effect until after the war in 1945. Sculpture was thus commissioned

*Joan Miró, "Nord-Sud", 1917,*
*oil on canvas, 62 × 70 cm.*

122

once again, finding its place in the architectural environment," concluded Jean-Louis Prat, director of the Foundation in the thirties.

On several occasions, the Foundation has also taken the opportunity to pay homage to Joan Miró, one of the artists at the origin of this project. Important exhibitions were devoted to him in 1968, 1973 and 1979, the last one being in 1990 with his painted work that had never before been presented in its entirety. Indeed, for the first time, collectors and museums from all over the world had accepted to lend, for the duration of a retrospective exhibition, works which until then, had never been shown in France and even, as far as some of them were concerned, had never been shown at all. In all, 120 works, paintings, gouaches and drawings were exhibited, including *Nord Sud, La Ferme, Carnaval d'Arlequin, Intérieur hollandais* and *Une Etoile caresse le sein d'une négresse.*

1. André Malraux, "Lettre à Roger Caillois", in catalogue *Le Musée imaginaire d'André Malraux,* Maeght éditeur, Paris, 1973.
2. Jean Leymarie, *Bonnard dans sa lumière,* collection Archives, Maeght éditeur, Paris, 1978.

123

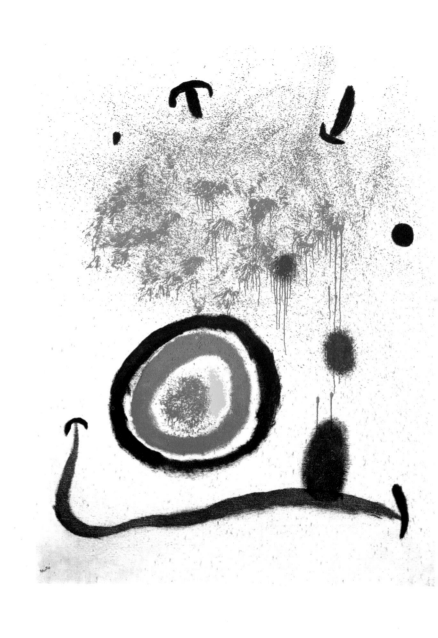

Joan Miró, "Naissance du jour I", 1964,
oil on canvas, 146 × 113.5 cm.

THE MARGUERITE AND AIMÉ MAEGHT FOUNDATION

# List of the exhibitions organised by the Maeght Foundation

**1964** "Inauguration de la Fondation Maeght" * .......... 28th July

**1966** "Dix ans d'art vivant 1945-1955" * ............... April-May
"Wassili Kandinsky", retrospective * .......... July-September

**1967** "Dix ans d'art vivant 1955-1965" * ................ May-July
"Hommage à Marc Chagall", retrospective * ... August-September

**1968** "Art vivant 1965-1968" * ....................... April-June
"Joan Miró", retrospective * ................ July-September
"Simon Hantaï" * ..................... December-January

**1969** "Alexander Calder", retrospective * ............... April-May
"Peintres-illustrateurs, livres illustrés modernes
depuis Manet" * .............................. June-July
"A la rencontre d'Henri Matisse"
Retrospective * ........................... July-September

**1970** "À la rencontre de Pierre Reverdy" * ............ March-April
"L'Art vivant aux Etats-Unis" * .............. July-September
"Jean-Paul Riopelle, grands formats" ...... December-January

**1971** "René Char" * ................................ April-May
"Une école, une fondation" ......................... June
"Hans Hartung, grands formats" * ............... June-July
"Hommage à Georges Rouault" * ........... July-September
"Paul Rebeyrolle" * .................... December-January

**1972** "Lars Fredrikson" * ...................... February-March
"Titina Maselli" * ................................ March
"Donation Gonzales" * ....................... June-July
"Nicholas de Staël", retrospective * .......... July-September
"Maeght éditeur" * ..................... December-January

**1973** "Jean-Claude Farhi" * .................... February-March
"Louis Le Brocquy" * ....................... March-April
"Joan Miró, sculptures et céramiques" * .......... April-June
"Le Musée imaginaire d'André Malraux" * .... July-September
"Bram Van Velde", retrospective * ........ December-January

125

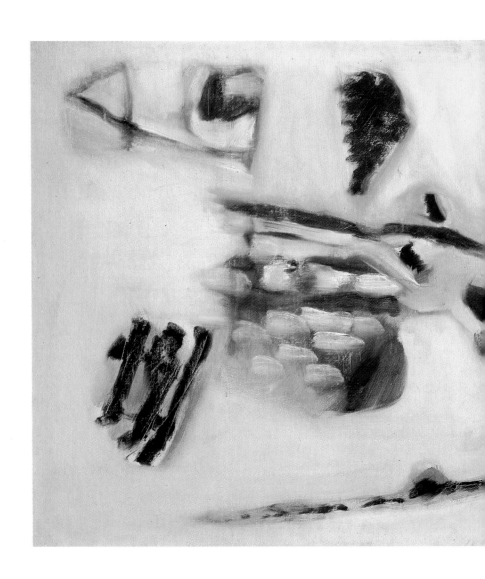

◀ Pierre Tal-Coat, *"Grand Tracé II"*, 1955,
*oil on canvas, 96 × 200 cm.*

---

■

**1974**   "Claude Garache" * . . . . . . . . . . . . . . . . . . . . . . . . February-March
"Pol Bury, 25 tonnes de colonnes" * . . . . . . . . . . . . March-May
"Zoltan Kemeny", retrospective * . . . . . . . . . . . . . . March-May
"X<sup>e</sup> anniversaire de la Fondation Maeght" * . . . July-September

**1975**   "L'Art graphique à la Fondation Maeght" * . . . . January-March
"Bonnard dans sa lumière", retrospective * . . . . July-September
"Louis Gosselin" * . . . . . . . . . . . . . . . . . . . . . . . December-January
"Jean-Luc et Titi Parant" * . . . . . . . . . . . . . . December-January

**1976**   "Daily Bul and Co" * . . . . . . . . . . . . . . . . . . . . February-March
"Henri Michaux", retrospective * . . . . . . . . . . . . . . . April-June
"Antoni Tàpies", retrospective * . . . . . . . . . . . . July-September
"Hommage à Gonzales" * . . . . . . . . . . . . . . . December-January

**1977**   "Jean-Michel Meurice" * . . . . . . . . . . . . . . . . January-February
"Jacques Monory - Opéras glacés" * . . . . . . . . January-February
"Marc Chagall. Livres. Gravures originales
    pour Aragon et Malraux" * . . . . . . . . . . . . . . . . . . . April-May
"Jean Messagier" * . . . . . . . . . . . . . . . . . . . . . . . . . . June-July
"Paul Klee", retrospective * . . . . . . . . . . . . . . . . July-September

**1978**   "Raoul Ubac", retrospective * . . . . . . . . . . . . . . . . . March-May
"Alberto Giacometti", retrospective * . . . . . . . . . July-September
"Georges Braque - Œuvre graphique" * . . . December-February

**1979**   "Saül Steinberg", retrospective * . . . . . . . . . . . . . . March-April
"Richard Lindner", retrospective * . . . . . . . . . . . . . . . May-June
"Joan Miró, peintures, dessins,
    sculptures 1956-1979" * . . . . . . . . . . . . . . . . . . July-September
"Bernard Moninot" * . . . . . . . . . . . . . . . . . . . . December-January

**1980**   "Dessins de la Fondation Maeght" * . . . . . . . . . . . . March-May
"Georges Braque", retrospective * . . . . . . . . . . . . . . July-October

**1981**   "Hommage à Pablo Picasso" . . . . . . . . . . . . . . . . . . . April-June
"Sculpture du XX<sup>e</sup> siècle : 1900-1945" * . . . . . . . . July-October

128

**1982** "L'Univers d'Aimé et Marguerite Maeght" *..... July-October
"Karel Appel et Pierre Alechinsky - Encres à deux
pinceaux" *.......................... December-January

**1983** "Anne Madden, peintures et papiers récents" * February-March
"Sam Francis, peintures et monotypes" *......... March-May
"Louis Cane, œuvres récentes" *................. May-June
"Max Ernst" *............................. July-October

**1984** "Hommage à Joan Miró, peintures,
sculptures, dessins" *........................ March-May
"Robert Rauschenberg, œuvres récentes" *......... May-June
"Marc Chagall, rétrospective
de l'œuvre peint" *........................ July-October

**1985** "FRAC, Provence-Alpes-Côte-d'azur,
deux ans d'acquisitions" *................ February-March
"Piet Mondrian" *............................ March-May
"Christo - Surrounded Islands", drawings,
plans, photos, models *........................ May-June
"Jean Dubuffet", retrospective *................ July-October

**1986** "Peintres-illustrateurs du XXᵉ siècle, Aimé Maeght, bibliophile"
200 original editions *........................ March-May
"Jasper Johns : l'œuvre graphique
100 œuvres de 1960-1985" *..................... May-June
"Un musée éphémère, collections privées
françaises, 1945-1985" *..................... July-October

**1987** "Jean Bazaine" *............................ March-April
"Domenico Gnoli", retrospective *................ May-June
"À la rencontre de Jacques Prévert" *......... July-October

**1988** "Cabinet des dessins de la Fondation Maeght" *.. March-May
"Le peintre et l'affiche : de Lautrec à Warhol" *.... May-June
"Fernand Léger", retrospective *............... July-October

**1989** "Arts de l'Afrique noire, collection Barbier-Mueller" * March-May
"L'Œuvre ultime : de Cézanne à Dubuffet" *.... July-October

**1990** "Un musée - une fondation, collection du musée
d'Art Moderne de Saint-Etienne" *......... February-March
"Jean-Paul Riopelle. D'hier et d'aujourd'hui" *.... April-June
"Joan Miró : rétrospective
de l'œuvre peint" *........................ July-October

129

**1991** "Cabinet des dessins de la Fondation Maeght" ... February-June
"Nicolas de Staël", rétrospective * ........... July-September

**1992** "Art millénaire des Amériques,
collection Barbier-Mueller" * ................... April-June
"L'Art en mouvement" * ..................... July-October

**1993** "Collection de la Fondation Maeght:
Un choix de 150 œuvres" * ................. July-October

**1994** "Trentième anniversaire de la Fondation Maeght
Georges Braque: rétrospective" * ............. July-October

**1995** "Bacon-Freud: Expressions" * ................. July-October

**1996** "Germaine Richier", rétrospective * ............ April-August

**1997** "La sculpture des peintres" * ............... July-November

**1998** "Cour Henri Laurens
Fonds Pierre Reverdy" ........................ May-June
"Otto Dix: Metropolis" * ..................... July-October

**1999** "Vision nouvelle d'une collection" * .......... July-November

**2000** "Sam Szafran" * ......................... February-April
"Paul Rebeyrolle" * .......................... April-June
"Le Nu au XXᵉ siècle" * ..................... July-October

**2001** "Joan Miró: Métamorphoses des formes" * ........ April-June
"Kandinsky", rétrospective * ................. July-October

**2002** "Miquel Barceló: Mapamundi" * ................ April-June
"Henri Moore", rétrospective * .............. July-November

**2003** "Arles et la photographie" * ................ February-March
"La Russie et les avant-gardes" * ............. July-November

130        *A catalogue was published for this exhibition.*

# THE FOUNDATION'S NIGHTS

VI

# nuits de la fondation maeght

saint-paul (a.m.)

## exposition de musique contemporaine

| trois concerts: | 4 août 21h30 | 5 août 21h30 | 7 août 21h30 |
|---|---|---|---|
| | quatuor parrenin<br>francis pierre, harpiste | yuji takahashi, pianiste | geneviève roblot, soprano |
| | œuvres de<br>berg, debussy, maderna<br>miroglio (1ère audition)<br>strawinsky | œuvres de<br>schönberg, cage<br>takemitsu (1ère audition)<br>boulez, messiaen<br>takahashi (1ère audition)<br>xenakis | ensemble instrumental<br>de musique contemporaine de paris<br>direction : konstantin simonovitch<br><br>œuvres de<br>varese, webern, philippot, kotonski<br>guézec, stockhausen |

prix des places : 30, 20, 15 et 5 f _ abonnement aux 3 concerts : réduction de 10%

| location : fondation maeght | guglielmi, piano | delrieu, disques | syndicat d'initiative | radio phonola | pathé-marconi | delbouis, disques |
|---|---|---|---|---|---|---|
| saint-paul<br>328163 | 8 rue lépante<br>nice<br>851624 | 45 av de la victoire<br>nice<br>886196 | 13 place masséna<br>nice<br>852522 | 42 bld desmoulins<br>monte-carlo<br>306526 | 5 bis pl du général de gaulle<br>antibes<br>340256 | 50 bld de la république<br>cannes<br>384459 |

Open to all forms of contemporary art, the Maeght Foundation has also been host to the world of music.

Each year, from 1965 and 1970, the *Nuits de la Fondation Maeght* were held in July and August in the Giacometti Courtyard. The organisation and programming were entrusted to the composer, Francis Miroglio, who met Aimé Maeght through Alexander Calder.

In March 1965, for the Ballets de l'Opéra de Marseille, Francis Miroglio composed the music for *Eppur si muove* by the choreographer Joseph Lazzini and asked Calder to create models of two stabiles and one mobile. At the end of the performances, the artist spoke to Francis Miroglio about the Maeght Foundation, inaugurated the previous year and suggested he visit the place.

"I saw and was dazzled, but I also heard, with the sound of the wind in the pines, the acoustic particularities of the Giacometti Courtyard. And the idea sprang to mind: what an ideal place to hold performances and to hear contemporary music [1]."

On his return to Paris, he met Aimé Maeght for the first time through his friends Calder and Jean Laude, and spoke to him about his project.

"You are anticipating my own wish to introduce music at the Foundation, but I think it's still too soon after the inauguration. 'Come back and see me later', was the art dealer's first reply."

When, a month later, the two men met again, Aimé Maeght still expressed reservations: "Too many things still need to be done at the Foundation before introducing music, but we shall definitely speak about it again."

Convinced that the undertaking would be a success, Francis Miroglio nevertheless produced three concert programmes, timed and costed, including first auditions of certain works, and presented them to Aimé Maeght the very next day.

In a few minutes, Aimé Maeght looked over the proposal, asked a few practical questions, reflected and then declared: "Excellent programmes. Let's do it. The best period is the end of July, beginning of August. We'll ask Miró to do the programme cover."

◀ Joan Miró, original poster for the "Nuits de la Fondation Maeght", 1965, lithograph, 88.5 × 55.5 cm.

133

The month of May was coming to an end, the undertaking was risky, but the enthusiasm and determination of Aimé Maeght carried it through. For its first anniversary, in July 1965, the Maeght Foundation opened its doors to contemporary music.

In an article published after Aimé Maeght's death in *La Quinzaine littéraire,* in October 1981, Francis Miroglio recalled: "These evenings presented many newly-created scores, written by the most important composers of our time, together with some key twentieth-century musical works, the interpretation of which often paved the way to a new approach or else introduced a reading giving a new insight. These world premières, with their meticulously prepared performances not only contributed to the Festival's reputation, but also took place before audiences whose sensitivity had been sharpened by the Museum's atmosphere, the sight of the paintings, the gently swaying mobiles, the pastel shadows cast by the sculptures on the terraces. (...) The arts of lyrics, poetry and theatre found in this setting a place in which to be read, room in which to be expressed, a stage on which they could be discussed. (...) Nonetheless, the vital element in this new development, born of the atmosphere of the *Nuits*, was the least spectacular, the part which the audience could not witness. Among the pine trees on the hill, sitting on the walls or watched by a music-loving minah-bird, composers conversed with painters, discussed with sculptors, poets emerged from their white obsession, choreographers expressed themselves with people working in theatre, black jazz artists opened up to European musicians.(...) As festivals went by, there was an intensification of the dynamic of collaboration and of merging between the different forms of artistic expression — music, plastic arts, poetry, dance, theatre, cinema — each of which had its own place among all the Foundation's activities (..)"

Looking through the programmes, whose covers were designed by painters and whose introductory texts were written by writers or poets, one can conjure up what was, at the time, a festival in a completely new vein, where different types of music mingled and where great composers and soloists first rose to fame in France.

## 1965

4th August: the Parrenin Quartet, with the harpist Francis Pierre, performed works by Berg, Debussy, Maderna, Miroglio, Schönberg and Stravinsky. 5th August: Yuji Takahashi, the Japanese pianist, performed works by Boulez, Cage, Messiaen, Xénakis and new compositions by Takemitsu and Takahashi.

134

7th August: the Ensemble Instrumental de Musique Contemporaine de Paris, conducted by Simonovitch, with the soprano Geneviève Roblot, performed works by Guezec, Kontonski, Philippot, Stockhausen, Varèse and Webern.

## 1966

31st July: the Ars Nova ensemble conducted by Marius Constant performed works by Ives, Ohana, Paccagnini, Schönberg and new compositions by Ballif and Trow.

2nd August: the Domaine Musical orchestra conducted by Gielen, with the soloist Yvonne Loriod, performed works by Webern and new compositions by Arrigo, De Pablo and Mefano.

3rd August: an ensemble of soloists performed for the first time works by Guyonnet, Miroglio, Stockhausen and Xénakis.

1st, 3rd, 5th, 6th and 7th August: the Merce Cunningham Dance Company, participating for the first time in a European festival, danced to music by John Cage, La Monte Young and Gordon Mumma.

*Aimé Maeght and John Cage in 1966.*

135

◄ Merce *Cunningham rehearsing in the Giacometti Courtyard in 1966.*

———————————————————■———————————————————

*From left to right: Merce Cunningham, John Cage,*
*Francis Miroglio, Carolyn Brown, Geneviève Roblot and Aimé Maeght*
*during the second festival of the "Nuits de la Fondation" in 1966.*

———————————————————■———————————————————

**1967**

An exhibition dedicated to René Char is held at the same time. The theatre makes its appearance.

3rd August, the pianist Claude Helffer interprets works by Berg, Webern, Amy, Bartok and creations by Bertoncini, Tremblay and Evangelisti.
4th August, the Sara Pardo company of contemporary dance gives four ballets to music by De Pablo, Gorecki, Webern and Varese.
5th August, readings of René Char's poems by the Jacques Guimet theatre company, directed by Francis Arnaud.

137

# NUITS DE LA
# FONDATION MAEGHT

SAINT-PAUL

## IIIe FESTIVAL INTERNATIONAL
## DE MUSIQUE ET D'ART CONTEMPORAINS

CONCERTS BALLETS POESIE CINEMA

10 CREATIONS ET 13 PREMIERES AUDITIONS

**3 Août 21 h 30**
CLAUDE HELFFER pianiste
Berg Webern Amy Bettinelli
Boucourechliev Evangelisti Barraqué

**4 Août 21 h 30**
COMPAGNIE DE DANSE
CONTEMPORAINE
SARA PARDO
Yves de Pablo Tudor Wolpe
Varèse Chica Varèse

**5 Août 21 h 30**
COMPAGNIE JACQUES GUIMET
RENE CHAR
Poète de la tendresse

**6 Août 21 h 30**
ENSEMBLE MUSIQUE
VIVANTE
GENEVIEVE ROBLOT soprano
Direction DIEGO MASSON
Shinohara Haubenstock Ramati
Clementi Nilsson Boulez

**9 Août 21 h 30**
QUATUOR A PERCUSSION
DE PARIS
VINKO GLOBOKAR trombone
Artaud Boucourechliev Globokar Xenakis

**10 Août 21 h 30**
SEVERINO GAZZELLONI flûtiste
BRUNO CANINO pianiste
Prokofiev Matsudaira Yun Castiglioni
Krenek Maderna

**11 Août 21 h 30**
ENSEMBLE ARS NOVA
DE L'ORTF
IVRY GITLIS violoniste
Direction ERNEST BOUR
Schoenberg Mestral Berio Amy
Koering Varèse

## Spectacle permanent
avec films sur
Bazaine Cage Calder Cesar Chagall Ernst
Etienne-Martin Hartung Kagel Michaux
Nono Stockhausen Stravinsky Viseux

---

**HOMMAGE A MARC CHAGALL DANS LES SALLES DU MUSEE ILLUMINE**

Prix des places (une soirée) concerts 24 F, T.P. Ballet 30 F, 35 F
Poésie 15 F, B.P. Abonnement réduit, 10 F
Cars spéciaux à la gare de Cannes et Nice. Parking assuré

Pour tous renseignements et locations s'adresser à

SAINT-PAUL    PARIS    NICE    CANNES    ANTIBES    JUAN-LES-PINS
Fondation Maeght    Fondation Maeght    Syndicat d'initiative    Agence Havas    Office du Tourisme    Office du Tourisme
Tél. 31 81 63    16 rue Berryer    Hôtel Agence Havas    17 rue Maréchal Foch    Place de Gaulle    Square Courbet
                Tél. 267 16 92    13 place Masséna    Tél. 93 00 73    Tél. 34 25 35    Tél. 61 04 41
                                Tél. 85 47 89

■

6th August: the Musique Vivante ensemble conducted by Diego Masson,
with the soprano Geneviève Roblot, performed works by Boulez and gave
first performances of works by Nilsson, Clementi, Haubenstock-Ramati
and Shinohara.

9th August: the Quatuor à percussions de Paris, with the trombonist
Globokar, played for the first time in France works by Rotter, Nono, Berio
Globokar and Brown.

10th August: the Italian flautist Severino Gazzelloni and the pianist Bruno
Canino gave a recital of works by Renosto, Matsudaira, Yun, Castiglioni,
Kontonski and Miroglio.

11th August: the Ars Nova ensemble conducted by Ernest Bour, with the
violinist Ivry Gitlis, performed works by Schönberg and Varèse and played
for the first time scores by Mestral, Benhamou and Koering.

Rehearsal by the Ars Nova ensemble, conducted by Ernest Bour,
for the concert on 11th August, 1967, in the Giacometti Courtyard.

139

■

◀ World première of *Tremplin* by Francis Miroglio in the Giacometti Courtyard, with special illumination of the orchestra, in 1969.

*Cecil Taylor and Aimé Maeght, 28th July, 1969.*

**1968**

22nd July: the Foundation presented the Concert Irregular by Joan Brossa, music by Carlos Santos, directed by Portabella, sets and costumes by Joan Miró.

**1969**

A projection of art and experimental films was included in the festival.

21st and 23rd July: the Musique vivante ensemble conducted by Diego Masson with four singers (Marie-Thérèse Cahn, Geneviève Roblot, Luis Masson and Jean-Marie Gourlou), performed the world premières of two musical theatre works by Haubenstock-Ramati and Miroglio, directed by Jacques Polieri, with projections of paintings by Alain Le Yaouanc. 22nd July: the Musique vivante ensemble and soloists conducted by Diego Masson performed Webern and Kagel in French premières and Arrigi, Guezec and De Pablo in world premières.

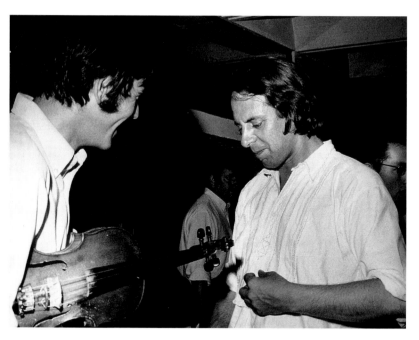

*The composer Karlheinz Stockhausen at the Foundation, 26th July, 1969.*

143

5th and 27th July: first performances of works by Ferrari and Koering.
26th July: four world premières of Karlheinz Stockhausen by Harold Boje, Roy Art, Michael Vetter and an ensemble of soloists.
28th and 29th July: Cecil Taylor and his group filled the Giacometti courtyard twice over with their tones.

## 1970

The exhibition "L'Art vivant aux États-Unis" took place at the same time as the festival and proposed programmes devoted to the American "underground" cinema as well as "events" by American artists.

16th July: the American composer and conductor Lukas Foss, heading the Evening for New Music Ensemble, performed Lukas Foss and Joël Chabade with a plastic "performance" by Robert Israël "M.A.P.".

Hans Walter Müller's experimental, inflatable theatre, installed during the "Nuits de la Fondation" in 1970.

145

———————————————————————————————————————————— ■ ————————————————————————————————————————————

17th, 18th, 19th, and 21st July: ballet and "events" by the Merce Cunningham Dance Company to music by Oliveros, Cage, Mumma and Tudor; sets by Jasper Johns, Robert Morris and Frank Stella.

20th July: the Ars Nova ensemble and the Evening for New Music Ensemble united for the world première performances of Hiller, Feldman, Brown, Foss and Reynolds.

22nd July: the Evening for New Music played works by Burge, Carter, Williams, Behrman, Budd and Albright in world or European premières. Various "performances" by Carl André, Hans Haake and Robert Whitman also took place on this occasion.

25th and 27th July: the Albert Ayler Sextet performed.

28th July: following Sylvia Monfort's initiative, general meetings for professionals were held, devoted to the question of theatrical creation in France.

29th July and 4th August: presence of La Monte Young and his unlimited frequencies.

3rd and 5th August: a concert by Sun Râ Arkestra gave the opportunity to hear extraordinary jazz in an experimental, inflatable theatre designed by Hans Walter Müller.

The *Nuits de la Fondation Maeght* consecrated a multiform creative activity. The audiences and spectators have retained lasting, brilliant memories of them. Unfortunately, such an undertaking was, from a simply financial point of view, too difficult for a private Foundation to sustain. In 1971, it was necessary to end the experiment, in spite of the success obtained in the defence and illustration of contemporary music.

After his father's death, Adrien Maeght attempted, in 1984, to rekindle the flames of the festival. He had, in particular, asked Strejinsky, an acoustician at Geneva University, to create a podium with large acoustic reflectors, thus avoiding the problems that had bothered the musicians and singers of the first *Nuits*. Over a period of five years, a new series of concerts gave the opportunity to hear, under the direction of Blaise Calame, some world creations of important composers, musicians and singers including Mstislav Rostopovitch, Luciano Berio, Jean-Claude Risset, Emmanuel Krivine, Frédéric Lodéon, Michel Portal, Margaret Price and Karlheinz Stockhausen. But, once again, it proved necessary to cede to the pressures of finance.

1. Francis Miroglio, Cahier du CREM.

*Aimé Maeght, amateur film-maker.*

THE MARGUERITE AND AIMÉ MAEGHT FOUNDATION

# ART FILMS

*"Raoul Ubac",*
*a scene from the film by Caroline Laure and Franco Lecca, 1972.*

Beginning in 1969, Aimé Maeght, who was fascinated by photography and cinema and surrounded by artists who had become his friends, decided to produce films devoted to art. Like the Foundation, open to art in all its diverse forms, Aimé Maeght explored, through the film camera, many different artistic domains. The motivation for such a choice was above all his intense interest in living art and his desire to share this passion.

Entrusting the making of these documentary films to different film-makers, Francesc Catala Roca, Clovis Prévost, Jean-Michel Meurice, Raoul Sangla, Ernst Scheidegger, or Carlos Vilarderbo, Aimé Maeght produced thirty or so short- and full-length films projected at the Foundation's cinema.

Thus the *Nuits de la Fondation* 1969 and 1970 were filmed. Film was the ideal means of capturing for ever a very special moment such as Cecil Taylor, Terry Riley, Albert Ayler or Sun Râ in concert.

Other films show the artists at work: Raoul Ubac tracing tracks in the sand, Alexander Calder directing, in a factory, the assembly of a monumental stabile, Joan Miró working on his Osaka ceramic mural in Japan.

Painters and sculptors also became, in their turn, film-makers. Pol Bury made, for example, several films, including *Une leçon de géométrie plane* or Valerio Adami who made *Vacances dans le désert*.

But the greatest success in this domain is probably the series of three full-length films made by André Malraux: *Les Métamorphoses du regard*. In three parts: *Les Dieux de la nuit et du soleil, Les Maîtres de l'irréel* and *Le Monde sans dieux*, the writer explored questions relating to the meaning of art from Lascaux to our time.

151

# List of Films

**NUITS DE LA FONDATION MAEGHT, 1969**

- *Free Jazz : Concert Cecil Taylor*
3 films 16 mm, colour, 26', 1969-70
1 film, 1 hour 30'
Directed by Raoul Sangla

- *Cette nuit là, les hommes marchèrent sur la Lune*
1 film 16 mm, colour, 18', 1969-70
Directed by Carlos Vilardebo

**NUITS DE LA FONDATION MAEGHT, 1970**

- *Free Jazz : Concert Lukas Foss*
1 film 16 mm, colour, 59', 1970
Directed by Jean-Michel Meurice

- *Film constat : Terry Riley*
1 film 16 mm, colour, 48', 1970
Directed by Jean-Michel Meurice

- *Albert Ayler : le dernier concert*
1 film 16 mm, colour, 51', 1970-71
Directed by Jean-Michel Meurice

- *Sun Râ*
1 film 16 mm, colour, 55', 1971
Directed by Jean-Michel Meurice

**EXHIBITION ART VIVANT AUX ÉTATS-UNIS**

- *Dans une heure et demain peut-être*
1 film 16 mm, colour, 52', 1970
Directed by Jean-Michel Meurice

**SOURCES DE L'ART CONTEMPORAIN**

- *La couleur de la revue blanche*
1 film 16 mm, colour, 13', 1965
Directed by Huguette Marquand-Ferreux

- *Gaudi*
1 film 16 mm, colour, 30', 1969-1970
Directed by Clovis Prévost

- *À bas les murs du silence (Les graffiti)*
1 film 16 mm, colour, 38', 1970
Directed by Clovis Prévost and William MacLean

152

• *Les Métamorphoses du regard*
— "Les Dieux de la nuit et du soleil"'
— "Les Maîtres de l'iréel"'
— "Le Monde sans Dieux"'
3 films 16 mm, colour, 3 × 52', 1974
With the participation of Pierre Dumayet and Walter Langlois
Directed by Clovis Prévost

**FILMS DEVOTED TO ARTISTS**

• JOSEP LLORENS ARTIGAS: *céramique*
1 film 16 mm, colour, 23', 1969
Directed by Francesc Catala Roca

• ALEXANDER CALDER: *portrait*
1 film 16 mm, colour, 40', 1971
Directed by Charles Chaboud

• MARC CHAGALL: *portrait*
Exhibition at the Grand Palais
1 film 16 mm, colour, 53', 1969
Directed by Pierre Dumayet

• ALBERTO GIACOMETTI:
1 film 16 mm, colour, 29', 1965-1966
Directed by Ernst Scheidegger and Peter Münger

• ZOLTAN KEMENY :
1 film 16 mm, colour, 1969
Directed by Charles Chaboud

• JOAN MIRÓ, JOSEP LLORENS ARTIGAS: *céramique murale (Osaka 1970)*
1 film 16 mm, colour, 12', 1970
Directed by Francesc Catala Roca

• JOAN MIRÓ: *peinture murale (Osaka 1970)*
1 film 16 mm, colour, 12', 1970
Directed by Francesc Catala Roca

• JOAN MIRÓ: *l'altre*
1 film 16 mm, colour, 29', 1970
Directed by Pere Portabella

• JOAN MIRÓ: *lithographie d'une affiche*
1 film 16 mm, colour, 18', 1971
Directed by Clovis Prévost

• JOAN MIRÓ: *sculpteur*
1 film 16 mm, colour, 38', 1973
Directed by Clovis Prévost and Carlos Santos

153

- JOAN MIRÓ:
1 film 16 mm, colour, 38', 1973
Directed by Franco Lecca and Caroline Laure

- JOAN MIRÓ: *Forzea, sculptures*
1 film 16 mm, colour, 30', 1973
Directed by Pere Portabella

- JOAN MIRÓ: *tapisserie*
1 film 16 mm, colour, 30'
Directed by Pere Portabella

JEAN-PAUL RIOPELLE: *portrait*
1 film 16 mm, colour, 24'
Directed by Pierre Schneider

- ANTONI TAPIES:
1 film 16 mm, 32', 1969-1970
Directed by Clovis Prévost

- RAOUL UBAC: *portrait*
1 film 16 mm, colour, 34', 1972
Directed by Caroline Laure and Franco Lecca

**FILMS MADE BY THE ARTISTS**

- *8500 tonnes de fer*
1 film 16 mm, black and white, 14', 1971
Directed by Pol Bury and Clovis Prévost

- *Une leçon de géométrie plane*
1 film 16 mm, black and white, 13', 1971
Directed by Pol Bury and Clovis Prévost

- *135 km/h*
1 film 16 mm, black and white, 16', 1972
Directed by Pol Bury and Clovis Prévost

- *Vacances dans le désert I et II*
2 films 16 mm, colour, 35', 1972
Directed by Gian Carlo and Valerio Adami.

154

# THE FOUNDATION'S
# PHOTOGRAPH ALBUM

Marguerite Maeght welcomes Nadia Léger,
on the evening of the inauguration, the 28th July, 1964.

*Duke Ellington and Joan Miró,
at the Foundation in 1966.*

The foundation's photograph album

◀ *Duke Ellington and Yoyo Maeght,*
*in July 1966.*

*Georges Braque and Isabelle Maeght*
*in 1963.*

The Foundation's photograph album

Marc Chagall, André Malraux and Aimé Maeght,
in front of "La Vie",
at the opening of "Hommage à Marc Chagall", in August 1967.

160

Marguerite Maeght, the publisher Tériade and his wife Alice, at the exhibition "Hommage à Marc Chagall", in 1967.

The Foundation's photograph album

*Marguerite Maeght, Marc Chagall and Nadia Léger.*

*Aimé Maeght, with Marc Chagall
and Vava Chagall,
preparing "Et sur la terre" by André Malraux,
in the engraving workshops in Saint-Paul.*

163

*Félix Zanutto and Simone Signoret at the Foundation in June 1967.*

*Aimé Maeght in front of "Marylin, 1967" by Andy Warhol during the exhibition "Art Vivant 1965-1968", in 1968.*

A *few hours before the opening of his retrospective* ▶
*at the Foundation, Alexander Calder installs*
*a stabile in the entrance garden.*

Max Ernst at the Maeght Foundation
*at the conference on kinetics, in 1969.*

*Sol Lewit installs "Five cubes", 1970,*
*white-painted steel, 450 × 450 × 160 cm,*
*for the exhibition "L'Art vivant aux États-Unis", in 1970.*

THE MARGUERITE AND AIMÉ MAEGHT FOUNDATION

*Aimé Maeght and Hans Hartung,*
*at the exhibition "Hans Hartung, grands formats", in 1971.*

The Foundation's photograph album

Jean-Louis Prat, the Foundation's Director,
M. and Mme Georges Pompidou and Aimé Maeght,
at the retrospective "Nicolas de Staël", in 1972.

■

Edgar Faure's visit to the Foundation, for the exhibition
"Le Musée imaginaire d'André Malraux", in September 1973.

The Foundation's photograph album

*Bram Van Velde, Samuel Beckett and Aimé Maeght
at the retrospective devoted to the painter in 1973.*

THE MARGUERITE AND AIMÉ MAEGHT FOUNDATION

Ben and Aimé Maeght at the opening
of the exhibition "Daily Bul and Co.", 7th February, 1976.

The Foundation's photograph album

*Aimé Maeght and Saül Steinberg,*
*at The Steinberg retrospective, 10th March, 1979.*

*Yoyo Maeght, Robert Rauschenberg and Adrien Maeght
at the opening of the Rauschenberg exhibition, in 1984.*

*Adrien Maeght, Valerio Adami and Louis Cane at the opening
of the exhibition "Louis Cane, œuvres récentes", 7th May, 1983.*

From left to right:
*Michel Guy, Jean-Louis Prat, Gustav Zumsteg,*
*Edmonde Charles-Roux, Emilio Miró, Isabelle and Adrien Maeght,*
*at the exhibition "Hommage à Joan Miró", in March, 1984.*

The Foundation's photograph album

*Adrien Maeght and Dominique Bozo*
*at the retrospective of the painted works of Joan Miró, in July, 1990.*

Isabelle Maeght and the grandson of Joan Miró, Emilio,
on the evening of the opening of the exhibition "Miró", in July, 1990.

179

*Marco Del Re, "Natura silente IX", 2002,
mixed technique on paper Népal, 100 X 121 cm.*

# APPENDICES

*Marguerite and Aimé Maeght at the Foundation, 1976.*

# Marguerite and Aimé Maeght

**Biographical reference dates:**

**1906**
Aimé Maeght born 27th April in Hazebrouk (Nord). Son of Alfred Maeght, railway employee, and Marthe Marguerite Maeght Roy. He is the eldest of a family of five children.

**1909**
Marguerite Devaye born 25th August in Cannes. Daughter of François Devaye and Anna Fassone, wholesale merchants. She is the youngest daughter in a family of three children.

**1914-1925**
Aimé Maeght's father dies in the war. The family house having been destroyed, his mother is repatriated by the Red Cross, with her children, to Lassalle (Gard).
A war orphan, Aimé Maeght studies at the junior high school in Nîmes. He is interested in modern music and plays in amateur orchestras.

**1926-1929**
After his studies at the technical high school in Nîmes, he becomes a lithographer-draughtsman and leaves for Cannes where he works at the Robaudy printing works. He meets Marguerite Devaye and marries her on 31st July 1928. Interested in advertising, he produces a large number of posters.

**1930**
Opening of the Imprimerie des Arts. Birth of their first son, Adrien, on 17th March.

**1932**
Marguerite and Aimé Maeght open, in the rue des Belges, a decoration shop selling radio sets. First meeting with Pierre Bonnard while working on a lithograph.

**1936**
The shop gradually becomes an art gallery, called the Arte gallery, where local artists: Domergues, Lartigue, Pastour, etc. are exhibited.

**1939-1940**
Mobilized by the Marines in Toulon, Aimé Maeght returns to Cannes after the Armistice.

183

**1941**

The couple make friends with Pierre Bonnard. Following his advice, Aimé Maeght devotes himself definitively to the profession of art publisher and art dealer.

**1942**

Birth of their second son, Bernard, on 2nd May.

**1943**

Meeting with Henri Matisse who is to paint many portraits of Marguerite Maeght.

**1945**

In October, Marguerite and Aimé Maeght open an art gallery under their name at 13, rue de Téhéran in Paris and managed by Jacques Kober. The inaugural exhibition is dedicated to Matisse.

Passionately interested in publishing, Aimé Maeght publishes the first works of the Pierre à Feu collection (illustrated anthologies of poems or prose pieces). This collection is later completed by monographs (Bazaine, Chagall, Kandinsky, Miró).

**1946**

Group exhibition: *Sur quatre murs*, with Bonnard, Matisse, Picasso, Braque, Léger, Rouault, Gris and others.

First important original edition: *Description d'un combat* by Franz Kafka, illustrated by Atlan.

Exhibition *Le noir est une couleur* whose catalogue constitutes the first issue of *Derrière Le Miroir (large-format journal illustrated with original lithographs and with texts by poets, writers and art critics).*

**1947**

First exhibition *Les mains éblouies*, which presents the new trends in painting and sculpture (Rezvani, Dmitrienko, Mason, Quentin etc.). Adrien Maeght takes over the publishing activities until 1957.

*Les Miroirs profonds* appears, the most important journal in the Pierre à Feu collection, dedicated to Matisse and already including texts by great writers of the time. Exhibition *Le Surréalisme*, organised by Marcel Duchamp and André Breton, an important and controversial event. Publication of *Le Vent des épines* by Jacques Kober, illustrated by Bonnard, Braque, Matisse and of *Cahier* by Georges Braque. First *Georges Braque* exhibition.

**1948**

First exhibitions of *Geer, Bram Van Velde* and *Joan Miró*.

Publication of *Perspectives* by Paul Éluard, illustrated by Albert Flocon and of *L'Album 13* by Joan Miró, Louis-Gabriel Clayeux becomes the

184

gallery's director, he is a friend of Léger, Ubac, Bazaine, Calder, Giacometti; these artists start working with the gallery.

Exhibition *L'Art abstrait* prepared by Michel Seuphor and André Farcy.

## 1950

The publishing activities become increasingly important: publication of *Parler seul* by Tristan Tzara, illustrated by Joan Miró, *Milarepa* and *Une aventure méthodique* by Pierre Reverdy, illustrated by Georges Braque. First *Marc Chagall*, *Alexander Calder* and *Raoul Ubac* exhibitions. Marguerite and Aimé Maeght buy some property in Saint-Paul. Last exhibition *Les Mains éblouies* (Arnal, Alechinsky, Corneille, Youngerman, Palazuelo, Chillida and others).

## 1951

*Wassili Kandinsky* exhibition.

First *Alberto Giacometti* exhibition. The exhibition *Tendance* is dedicated to young artists (Germain, Pallut, and Poliakoff, amongst others).

## 1953

After a long illness, Bernard, Marguerite and Aimé Maeght's youngest son, dies on 25th November. Greatly distressed by this painful ordeal, they withdraw to Saint-Paul. The affection and the presence of their artist friends help them overcome their grief. They first have the idea of creating a meeting place for artists in Saint-Paul.

## 1953-1958

Paule and Adrien's wedding takes place on 8th April, 1954.

Birth of Isabelle (1955) and Florence (1956), daughters of Paule and Adrien Maeght.

During this period, the Paris gallery exhibits new artists: Saül Steinberg (1953), Pierre Tal-Coat (1954), Pablo Palazuelo (1955), Eduardo Chillida (1956), Ellsworth Kelly (1958) and François Fiedler (1959).

These artists, of different nationalities, join the Maeght gallery in a close form of collaboration never to be compromised, either in their work or their friendship.

Adrien Maeght leaves the gallery in 1958 and opens his own boockshop-art gallery at 42, rue du Bac in the 7th district in Paris.

## 1959-1961

Aimé Maeght opens his lithography and engraving workshops in Levallois. His whole life is now to focus on the creation and spreading of this new way of publicizing contemporary art. He later becomes one of its greatest promoters and also a great bibliophilist.

For the first time, Adrien Maeght exhibits the collages of his friend Jacques Prévert.

Birth of Yoyo (1959), third daughter of Paule and Adrien Maeght.

185

**1962-1963**

Marguerite and Aimé Maeght finance the construction of their Foundation in Saint-Paul. Its architect is Josep Lluis Sert.
Exhibition *Der Blaue Reiter* in 1962.

**1964**

Recognised as being in the public interest, the Maeght Foundation is inaugurated on 28th July by André Malraux who has backed this large-scale project. Marguerite and Aimé Maeght give a part of their collection to the Foundation which they will continue to add to throughout their lives.
Aimé Maeght receives the order of Chevalier de la Légion d'honneur.

**1965**

First *Nuits de la Fondation*. These evenings will take place every year in July until 1970.
The workshops in Levallois, being too small, are moved to the Arte printing house created by Adrien Maeght in rue Daguerre in the 14th district in Paris. Thus, the artists can now make use of the techniques of engraving, lithography, collotype, offset etc.

**1966**

First issue of *L'Éphémère* (a quarterly literary journal), led by Yves Bonnefoy, André du Bouchet, Gaëtan Picon, Michel Leiris, Louis-René des Forêts, Paul Celan and Jacques Dupin.
Exhibition *L'Art vivant* 1945-1955 at the Foundation.

**1967**

First exhibitions of *Paul Reyberolle* and *Antoni Tàpies*.
Retrospective exhibition of *Marc Chagall* at the Foundation.
Retransmission by Telstar of *"Notre Monde"*, the first programme broadcast by satellite in 53 countries. It includes a sequence about the Foundation and a ballet by Joseph Lazzini to music by Francis Miroglio.

**1968**

Publication of the first issue of *L'Art vivant*, a monthly review, essentially devoted to avant-garde research in the fields of plastic arts, cinema, photography, music and architecture.
Birth of Julien, son of Paule and Adrien Maeght.

**1969**

Aimé Maeght decides to produce films devoted to artists. Amongst the most important, a series of three full-length films: *Les Métamorphoses du regard* by André Malraux, co-produced by French Television.
First exhibition of *Pol Bury*.
Exhibition *À la rencontre de Matisse* at the Foundation.

**1970**
Publication of the first volume of the *Monographies* collection.
First *Valerio Adami* exhibition.

**1971**
Publication of the first part of *L'Art abstrait* by Michel Seuphor and Michel Ragon (5 volumes).
Publication of *Fêtes* by Prévert, illustrated by Alexander Calder.
Exhibition of *René Char* at the Foundation

**1972**
Retrospective exhibition of *Nicholas de Staël* at the Foundation.
Creation of the Pierre Reverdy committee at the Foundation.

**1973**
Important exhibition devoted to the *Musée imaginaire d'André Malraux* at the Foundation, which he inaugurates on 13th July.
Creation of the Placard series, which presents an artist's lithograph or silk-screen print with a poet's text.
Publication of *L'Unique* by Hölderlin, illustrated by Bram Van Velde.

**1974**
Inauguration of the Maeght gallery in Barcelona.
Organisation at the Foundation of the *Moments musicaux* which present young soloists (Augustin Dumay, Frédéric Lodéon, Emmanuel Krivine, Michel Portal, Henri Barda and Alain Planès, amongst others).
Inauguration of the Sainte-Roseline chapel in Les Arcs (Var), whose restoration is financed by Marguerite Maeght and which houses works by Marc Chagall, Diego Giacometti, Raoul Ubac and Jean Bazaine.

**1975**
In parallel with the review *Argile*, a collection of the same name is launched with the aim of promoting young authors illustrated by contemporary artists.
First *Claude Garache* exhibition.
Retrospective exhibition: *Bonnard dans sa lumière* at the Foundation.
Marguerite Maeght is awarded the order of Chevalier de la Légion d'honneur.
Publication of *Adonidès* by Jacques Prévert, illustrated by Joan Miró.
Project to create a centre in Paris which would group all the activities of the gallery, the publishing house and the Foundation and which would encourage experimental publishing and preserve certain artistic professions.
The huge project of restoring and rehabilitating a block of buildings in

187

the Marais was never to be finalised due to administative difficulties.
Film made by French television: *Du côté de chez les Maeght*, ten programmes of 26 minutes each, broadcast on the third channel.

## 1976

*Maeght publications* continues to publish many important original editions, lithographs, etchings and current publications.
First *Jacques Monory* exhibition.

## 1977

✝ Marguerite Maeght dies on 31st July.
Retrospective *Paul Klee* exhibition at the Foundation.
First *Shusaka Arakawa* and *Richard Lindner* exhibitions.
Publication of two books illustrated by Marc Chagall: *Et sur la terre* by André Malraux and *Celui qui dit les choses sans rien dire* by Louis Aragon.

## 1978

First *Gérard Titus-Carmel* exhibition.
Retrospective *Alberto Giacometti* exhibition at the Foundation.
Publication of *Petrificada petrificante* by Octavio Paz, illustrated by Antoni Tàpies.

## 1979

Inauguration of the new exhibition rooms at 14, rue de Téréhan, to present experimental and research work done by young artists (Paul Rotterdam, Peter Stämpfli, Hervé Télémaque, Nigel Hall and others).
First *Edward Kienholz* exhibition.

## 1980

First *Konrad Klapheck* exhibition.
Retrospective *Georges Braque* exhibition.

## 1981

First *Pierre Alechinsky, Isamu Noguchi* and *Takis* exhibition.
Retrospective: *La Sculpture du XXᵉ siècle: 1900-1945* at the Foundation.
✝ Aimé Maeght dies on 5th September.

188

# Chronology of the Foundation's construction

**1953**

• Marguerite and Aimé Maeght decide to create a meeting place for artists in Saint-Paul.

**1956**

• Aimé Maeght visits Joan Miró's studio in Palma de Majorca, built during 1955 and 1956 by Josep Lluis Sert.
Decides to choose Josep Lluis Sert as the architect for the Foundation.

**1957**

• 3rd June: Aimé Maeght sends Josep Lluis Sert a letter asking him to be the architect of his museum.
• 10th June: Josep Lluis Sert, being enthusiastic about the project, agrees. Starting point of a correspondence between the two men.
• December: Aimé Maeght's visit to the United States where he meets Josep Lluis Sert.

**1958**

• 2nd February: Josep-Luis Sert roughs out the first sketches.
• July: Josep Lluis Sert's visit to Saint-Paul.
• 10th November: first rough sketch for the building.
• 2nd December: second rough sketch for the building.

**1959**

• 6th June: planning permission asked for.
• July: first scale models of the Foundation.
• 15th-23rd July: Josep Lluis Sert visits Saint-Paul.
• 14th August: planning permission granted: n° 21 472.
• 7th October: Emmanuel Bellini's firm put in charge of the contract.

189

## 1960

- 5th January: Eugène Lizero and Emmanuel Bellini are named contract architects.
- 11th March: final plans for the museum.
- 2nd June: final plans for the chapel.
- 21st June: second series of plans for the director's house.
- 15th July: quotation for excavation work and shell.
- 5th September: work begins.
- 22nd October: first foundations of all the museum rooms.
- 20th November: museum's foundations completely finished.
- 22nd December: changes in the plans to the falsework and equipment of the chapel.

## 1961

- 26th April: plans of the caretaker's house.
- July: Josep Lluis Sert visits France; works with the artists and particularly with Joan Miró.
- August: cathedral in wood for the construction of the half-moons in the "Mairie".
- 22nd September: third series of plans for the director's house.
  Completion of the two great monitors, dismantled and covered with a cocoon.
  Problem of heating.
- 1st December: excavation of the labyrinth almost finished.

## 1962

- 1st to 5th January: Huson Jackson, Sert's partner, visits Saint-Paul.
- February: Aimé Maeght visits the United States.
- 1st June: screen wall of the "Mairie" completed.
- 19th June: building site cleaned up, installation of rails for lighting.
- 7th to 22nd July: Aimé Maeght, Josep Lluis Sert and Joan Miró in Saint-Paul.
- 12th July: painting of the museum and the director's house, interior and exterior electric lighting.
- July: installation of the models of Joan Miró's sculptures in the labyrinth.
- 24th August: Josep Lluis Sert in Saint-Paul again.
- 25th October: the director's house is completed.
  Water recycling system completed; completion of electrical work.

**1963**

- 16th to 23rd February: Josep Lluis Sert visits Saint-Paul.
- 9th August: final detailed accounts of the construction work.
- 22nd October: all the plasterwork has to be redone. Stained-glass windows and Raoul Ubac's Stations of the Cross installed.
- November: labyrinth sculptures completed.
- Ronald Gourley leaves the firm which takes the name "Sert, Jackson et Associés".

**1964**

- 15th May: donation of works and money to the Foundation, in the presence of a lawyer, by Marguerite and Aimé Maeght.
- Beginning of July: Josep Lluis Sert is in Saint-Paul; verification of final details.
- 18th July: the Foundation is recognised as being in the public interest.
- 28th July: inauguration of the Marguerite and Aimé Maeght Foundation by André Malraux, French Minister for Cultural Affairs.

191

# Artisans involved in the construction of the Foundation

Design Architect: Josep Lluis Sert, assisted by Huson Jackson and Ronald Gourley, Cambridge, United States.

Site Architects: Emmanuel Bellini and Eugène Lizero, Cannes.

Joan Miró's monumental ceramic creations were executed by Josep Llorens Artigas and Joan Gardy Artigas in Gallifa, Spain.

The mosaics of Georges Braque, Marc Chagall and Pierre Tal-Coat were executed by Lino Melano.

The stained-glass windows by Georges Braque and Raoul Ubac were made by Charles Marcq and the Ateliers Simon in Reims.

The bronze furniture, lampstands, benches and doorhandles were created by Diego Giacometti in Paris.

Joan Miró's fork was cast by the Etablissements Susse in Paris and his arrow was forged by the Atelier Demarquoy in Antibes.

Joan Miró's Grand Arc was executed by M. Venturi for the Etablissements Triverio in Nice.

The gardens were laid out by Fish, in Vallauris, under the direction of Albert Varey, Head Gardener of the Foundation.

# Principal donations to the Maeght Foundation

## WORKS DONATED BY THE ARTISTS

VALERIO ADAMI
- *Sigmund Freud in Viaggio verso Londra,* 1973
Acrylic on canvas
130 × 97 cm

- *Dessin,* 1979
Umbra, casein, pastel and pencil
187 × 142 cm
(Donated: 1979)

- *Dessin,* 1979
Sienna, casein, pastel and pencil
192 × 142 cm
(Donated: 1979)

JOSEP LLORENS ARTIGAS
AND JOAN MIRÓ
- 9 ceramics
Cf. Miró

POL BURY
- *Quatre-vingt-deux cordes verticales et leurs cylindres,* 1973
Wood and nylon
310 × 150 × 67.5 cm
(Donated: 1974)

- *Untitled,* 1978
11 Indian inks
(Donated: 1978)

- *Fontaine,* 1978
Stainless steel
230 × 410 × 270 cm
(Donated: 1978)

ALEXANDER CALDER
- *Une boule noire, une boule blanche,* 1930
Mobile
Height: 242 cm
(Donated by the artist and M. and A. Maeght, 1973)

- *Ten Restless Disks,* 1933
Stabile-mobile
400 × 300 cm
(Donated by the artist and M. and A. Maeght, 1973)

- *Eléphant,* 1930-1944
Bronze
Height: 14.5 cm
(Donated by the artist and M. and A. Maeght, 1973)

- *Danseuse,* 1930-1944
Bronze
Height: 68.5 cm
(Donated by the artist and M. and A. Maeght, 1973)

193

• *Chat,* 1930-1944
Bronze
Height: 13 cm
(Donated by the artist and
M. and A. Maeght, 1973)

• *Haltérophile,* 1930-1944
Bronze
Height: 21 cm
(Donated by the artist and
M. and A. Maeght, 1973)

• *Étoile de mer,* 1930-1967
Bronze
Height: 63 cm
(Donated by the artist and
M. and A. Maeght, 1973)

• *Cheval II*, 1930-1944
Bronze
Height: 10 cm
(Donated by the artist and
M. and A. Maeght, 1973)

• *Acrobates*, 1930-1944
Bronze
Height: 51.5 cm
(Donated by the artist and
M. and A. Maeght, 1973)

• *Empennage*, 1954
Stabile-mobile
150 × 240 cm
(Donated by the artist: 1968)

• *Trois soleils jaunes*, 1965
Mobile
233 × 100 cm
(Donated by the artist and
M. and A. Maeght, 1973)

ALAN DAVIE _____
• *The Horse that has Visions of
Immortality n° 1,* 1963
Oil on canvas
210 × 170 cm
(Donated: 1967)

HÉLÈNE DELPRAT _____
• *Untitled,* 1989
Acrylic on canvas
200 × 200 cm
(Donated: 1989)

MARCO DEL RE _____
• *La muse qui m'amuse,* 1991
Oil and combustion on wood
3 × 250 × 150 cm
(Donated: 1991)

PIERRE DMITRIENKO _____
• *Il Fuerte O*, 1967-1968
Oil on canvas
196 × 132 cm

EUGÈNE DODEIGNE _____
• *Le Pot de Fer*, 1965
Charcoal on paper
110 × 77.5 cm

CHRISTIAN DOTREMONT _____
• 6 drawings
Crayon on paper
27 × 21 cm
(Donated: 1978)

PIERRE FAUCHER _____
• *La Selva,* 1990
Acrylic and ink on canvas
200 × 200 cm
(Donated: 1990)

194

FRANÇOIS FIEDLER _____

• *Peinture*, 1965
Oil on canvas
196 × 132 cm
(Donated: 1967)

JEAN-MICHEL FOLON _____

• *Rake's Progress,* 1980
Indian ink on paper
54.5 × 84.5 cm

LARS FREDRIKSON _____

• *Structure dynamique*, 1969
Mixed technique
151 × 102 cm
(Donated: 1978)

• *Incurve IV*, 1971
Stainless steel and Plexiglas
100 × 175 cm
(Donated: 1972)

JOAN GARDY-ARTIGAS _____

• *Untitled*
Epoxy sculpture
200 × 50 × 50 cm

GÉRARD GASIOROWSKI _____

• *Pot de fleurs 29-30*, 1975
Acrylic on paper
74 × 61 cm
(Donated: 1985)

LIONEL GODART _____

• *Feux nocturnes*
Charcoal, spray and Indian ink
on canvas
102.5 × 89 cm
(Donated: 1980)

ROBERTA GONZALES _____

• Collection of 45 drawings
(Donated: 1972)

• *Le Jugement de Pâris*, 1952
Oil on canvas
146 × 97 cm
(Donated: 1972)

• *Les Flèches n° 2*, 1968
Oil on canvas
114 × 146 cm
(Donated: 1972)

• *La Fenêtre était grande
ouverte n° 1*, 1970
Oil on canvas
114 × 146 cm
(Donated: 1972)

HANS HARTUNG _____

• *T. 1971 - H. 13*, 1971
Acrylic on canvas
154 × 250 cm
(Donated: 1980)

• *P. 10 - 1980 - H. 8*, 1980
Charcoal on paper pasted down
on cardboard
51.4 × 36.3 cm
(Donated: 1980)

• *P. 25 - 1980 - H. 5*, 1980
Soft lead pencil and charcoal
on paper pasted down on
cardboard
56.6 × 76.8 cm
(Donated: 1980)

BARBARA HEPWORTH _____

• *Figure (Walnut)*, 1964
Bronze
Height: 181 cm
(Donated: 1967)

195

ALEXANDER ISRATI _____

• *Peinture*, 1974
Oil on canvas
200 × 180 cm
(Donated: 1977)

AKI KURODA _____

• *Weeping through the light,*
1991
Acrylic on canvas
270 × 160 cm (Donated: 1991)

DOMINIQUE LABAUVIE _____

• *Flying Saucer II*, 1991
Charcoal on paper
102.5 × 153 cm
(Donated: 1991)

LADISLAS KIJNO _____

• *Tic, Tac, Dou,* 1965
Oil on canvas
195 × 153 cm
(Donated: 1967)

NORBERT KRICKE _____

• Spatial sculpture:
*Grosse Fliessende*, 1965
Stainless steel
105 × 502 × 315 cm
(Donated: 1967)

ALAIN LE YAOUANC _____

• *E. E. M.*, 1966
Collage and gouache on paper
remounted on wood
80 × 80 cm
(Donated: 1968)

• *Masse dôme*, 1967
Assembly on wood
126 × 100 cm
(Donated: 1968)

ANNE MADDEN _____

• *Alignement*, 1972
Acrylic on canvas
Twice 162 × 228 cm

JEAN MESSAGIER _____

• *Une chaleur*, 1976
Oil on canvas
230 × 191 cm
(Donated: 1977)

HENRI MICHAUX
and Galerie Le Point Cardinal _____

• *Untitled*, 1974
Indian ink and coloured ink on
paper
51.5 × 65.5 cm
(Donated: 1976)

• *Untitled*, 1975
Indian ink and coloured ink on
paper
57 × 75 cm
(Donated: 1976)

JOAN MIRÓ _____

• *Femme et oiseau I*, 1964
Oil on canvas
199 × 199 cm

• *Femme et oiseau II*, 1964
Oil on canvas
199 × 199 cm

• *Naissance du jour I*, 1964
Oil on canvas
146 × 113.5 cm

• *Naissance du jour II*, 1964
Oil on canvas
162 × 130 cm

• *Naissance du jour III*, 1964
Oil on canvas
162 × 130 cm

*Vol d'oiseau à la première
étincelle de l'aube*, 1964
Oil on canvas
162 × 130 cm

• *Femme oiseau*, 1964
Oil on canvas
162 × 130 cm

• *Le Chant de la prairie*, 1964
Oil on canvas
193.5 × 130 cm

• Collection of 73 drawings
(Donated: 1979)

• *Oiseau solaire*, 1968
Carrara marble
157 × 240 × 137 cm
(Donated by the artist and
M. and A. Maeght, 1968)

• *Oiseau lunaire*, 1968
Carrara marble
300 × 260 × 120 cm
(Donated by the artist and
M. and A. Maeght, 1968)

• *Oiseau*, 1968
Wrought iron
130 × 182 × 128 cm
(Donated by the artist and
M. and A. Maeght, 1968)

• *Femme à la chevelure
défaite*, 1968
Carrara marble
210 × 150 × 90 cm
(Donated by the artist and
M. and A. Maeght, 1968)

• *Vitrail I et II*, 1979
Executed by the Ateliers Simon-
Charles Marcq, Reims
200 × 360 cm
(Donated by the artist and
M. and A. Maeght, 1980)

• *Tapisserie*, 1980
270 × 480 cm
(Donated: 1981)

• *8 maquettes arc de
la Fondation*, 1963
Ceramics

• *Tête de taureau*, 1970
Ceramic

• *Plaques murales*, 1963
The Maeght Foundation Tower
Ceramic

• *Gargouille*, 1964
Ceramic
90 × 40 × 50 cm
(Donated by the artist, Josep
Llorens Artigas and M. and
A. Maeght, 1968)

197

• *Gargouille*, 1968
Ceramic
95 × 40 × 50 cm
(Donated by the artist, Josep
Llorens Artigas and M. and
A. Maeght, 1968)

• *Céramique ronde
(Cadran solaire)*, 1973
Diametre: 310 cm
(Donated by the artist, Josep
Llorens Artigas and
M. and A. Maeght, 1973)

• Mur de la Fondation
Maeght, 1968
Ceramic
1240 × 200 cm
(Donated by the artist, Josep
Llorens Artigas and
M. and A. Maeght, 1973)

• Personnage, 1968
Ceramic
100 × 50 × 60 cm

• Personnage, 1968
Ceramic
90 × 30 cm

• Personnage (totem), 1968
Ceramic and iron
550 × 80 cm

• Ensemble de 70 gouaches

JOAN MITCHELL _____
• Mon paysage, 1967
Oil on canvas
260 × 180 cm
(Donated: 1980)

JACQUES MONORY _____
• Pompeï, 1971
Acrylic on canvas
3 × 195 × 130 cm
(Donated: 1977)

GÉRARD TITUS-CARMEL _____
• Neuf Constructions
éphémères, 1980
Black lead and red chalk on
paper
121 × 80 cm
(Donated: 1980)

RAOUL UBAC _____
• 8 fusains, 1977
200 × 50 cm
(Donated: 1978)

BRAM VAN VELDE _____
• Untitled, 1963
Gouache
120 × 125 cm
(Donated: 1973)

VLADIMIR VELICKOVIC _____
• Exit figure IX, 1980
Oil on canvas
200 × 140 cm
(Donated: 1980)

CLAUDE VISEUX _____
• Un prédateur, 1965
Stainless steel
105 × 245 cm
(Donated by the artist and the
Galerie
Le Point Cardinal, 1967)

198

## OTHER DONATIONS

**Mᵐᵉ Arp**

JEAN ARP _____
• *Pépin géant,* 1937-1966
Polished bronze
162 × 127 × 77 cm


**Comité Reverdy**

FRANCESCO DOMINGO _____
• *Portrait de Reverdy,* 1923
Charcoal on paper,
36.8 × 29.2 cm

• *Portrait de Reverdy,* 1923
Pencil on paper,
47 × 31.5 cm


**Bulgarian Government**

ENTCHOV PIRONKOV _____
• *Untitled*
Oil on canvas,
120 × 59.5 cm
(Donated: 1966)


**Galerie de France**

CHRISTIAN DOTREMONT _____
• *Journée détournée du temps,*
1974
Indian ink on paper
55.4 × 76.2 cm

• Pas un logogramme de bon
sens, 1974
Indian ink on paper
76.2 × 55.4 cm

**Galerie Le Dessin**

FRANÇOIS MARTIN _____
• *Fin de repas,* 1974
Indian ink on silk paper,
64.6 × 48.8 cm


**Galerie Le Point Cardinal**

Cf. Artists' donations, Henri
Michaux


**Mᵐᵉ Gonzales**

JOAN GONZALES _____
• Collection of 40 pastels,
gouaches, charcoal drawings
and water colours
(Donated: 1972)

**JULIO GONZALES** _____
• Collection of 50 pastels,
gouaches, charcoal drawings
and water colours
(Donated: 1972)

• *Standing figure*, 1932 -1935
Iron,
128 × 69 cm

• *Portrait de la poétesse
Jean de Neyreïs,* 1914-1918
Bronze,
21.5 × 20 × 12 cm
(Donated: 1972)

199

- *Daphné*, 1930-1936
Bronze,
142 × 70 × 35 cm
(Donated: 1972)

HANS HARTUNG _____
- *T. 51-9*, 1951
Oil on canvas,
97 × 146 cm
(Donated: 1972)

**Michel Guy**

BRAM VAN VELDE _____
- *Composition abstraite*, 1938
Oil on canvas
147 × 1,134 cm

- Composition abstraite, 1954
Oil on paper
186 × 148 cm

- *Composition abstraite*, 1957
Gouache
137 × 148.5 cm

- *Composition abstraite*, 1966
Oil on canvas
193 × 127.5 cm

**Mᵐᵉ Kandinsky**

WASSILI KANDINSKY _____
- *Le Nœud rouge*, 1936
Oil on canvas
89 × 116 cm
(Donated: 1966)

**M. Maurice Lefèvre-Foinet**

JACQUES VILLON _____
- *Luxembourg : étude*, 1935
Indian ink and pencil on paper
31.5 × 44.7 cm

CLAIRE FALKENSTEIN _____
- *Points*, 1965
Welded metal
150 × 95 × 65 cm
(Donated: 1968)

RUTH FRANKEN _____
- *Téléphone V*, 1967
Stainless steel, aluminium,
glass, electronic installation
30 × 30 × 30 cm
(Donated: 1968)

ALBERTO GIACOMETTI _____
- *Figures*, 1963
Catalogue heightened with
drawings
Black lead and ballpoint pen
on paper
22 × 37 cm
(Donated: 1976)

FERNAND LÉGER _____
- *Céramique*, 1953
100 × 195 cm
(Donated: 1976)

HENRI MATISSE _____
- *Portrait de Fabiani*, 1943
Pencil on paper
53 × 40.6 cm
(Donated: 1980)

200

**M<sup>me</sup> Léger**

FERNAND LÉGER ⎯⎯⎯⎯⎯⎯⎯⎯

• *Sculpture*
Bronze,
42 × 35 cm
(Donated: 1972)

• *Paysage aux oiseaux*, 1954
Gouache on paper
49 × 76 cm

• *Halles*, 1965
Indian ink drawing on paper
42 × 82 cm

**M<sup>me</sup> Tàpies**

ANTONI TÀPIES ⎯⎯⎯⎯⎯⎯⎯⎯

• *Charnière*, 1977
Imprints, pencil and solid
matter on paper
36.5 × 50.5 cm

• *Épingle à nourrice*, 1977
Pencil and collage on paper
37.5 × 50.5 cm

• *Flacon*, 1979
Pencil, acrylic and chalk on
paper
36 × 50.8 cm

**M<sup>me</sup> Reverdy**

JUAN GRIS ⎯⎯⎯⎯⎯⎯⎯⎯

• *Portrait de Pierre
Reverdy*, 1918
Pencil on cardboard
60 × 40.5 cm
(Donated: 1975)

**M<sup>me</sup> de Wendel**

LUIS FERNANDEZ ⎯⎯⎯⎯⎯⎯⎯⎯

• *Nature morte*
Pencil and Indian ink
on paper
50 × 64.4 cm

**M. Lauren Steingrim**

JEAN GROTH ⎯⎯⎯⎯⎯⎯⎯⎯

• *Dessin*, 1975
Indian ink on paper
87 × 60 cm
(Donated: 1975)

**M<sup>me</sup> Ossip Zadkine and M<sup>me</sup> Susse**

OSSIP ZADKINE ⎯⎯⎯⎯⎯⎯⎯⎯

• *Statue pour un jardin*, 1958
Bronze n° 2/6
253 × 112 × 57 cm

201

# Statutes of the Foundation

$T$he Marguerite and Aimé Maeght Foundation is a true Foundation. It is not dependent upon the administration of the national museums and is not subsidised in any way by the State. It was entirely financed by Marguerite and Aimé Maeght. This legal situation, a result of the statute laws of the Council of State, allows the founders to nominate, while living, an intellectually sound, autonomous legal entity to whom are bequeathed, by notarial act, the assets, furniture and estate by right and the administration of which they are responsible for in the public interest.

The Foundation, the duration of which is unlimited, aims to receive, acquire, restore, preserve and exhibit works of art to the public. It must also enable artists to meet and work together. The statutes stipulate that the Foundation encompass conferences, colloquiums, concerts, film projections and all artistic and cultural events. It is governed by a Board of Directors — presided by Adrien Maeght since the death of his father on 5th September 1981 — which is responsible for the representation of the Foundation in all facets of public life. It is composed of eleven voluntary members — nominated for nine years and three of whom are renominated every three years — designated by the founders, and of members representing the French Ministry of the Interior and the Ministry of Culture.

All the Board of Directors' decisions, in particular, the rights of transfer of property, the annual budget, the acceptance of donations and legacies must be approved by the competent Ministries. The Foundation's Director oversees the execution of the Board's decisions and is responsible for the various events.

The Foundation's Board of Directors also supports and encourages an independent association, the *Association des Amis de la Fondation Maeght* (The Friends of the Maeght Foundation Society) which contributes to the permanent collection.

The Foundation was built on land belonging to Marguerite and Aimé Maeght, who let it on a long-term lease. After the death of Marguerite Maeght in 1977, Adrien Maeght, who had inherited the land and the buildings, transformed this lease into a donation.

For very many years Marguerite and Aime Maeght helped the Foundation financially when it was necessary. Gradually, the budget balanced out and the deficit was paid off in 1983.

The total financial autonomy of the Foundation allows it to ensure its functioning and its exhibitions. It welcomes more than 250,000 visitors every year. All the works acquired or donated are part of the Foundation's heritage and are thus inalienable, as are the building and the land it stands on.

# Foundation's Key Figures

- The Foundation is 800 m outside Saint-Paul, 12 km front the Nice-Côte d'Azur airport, 80 km from Italy and 980 km from Paris.

- Surface area of the land: 10,540 m.

- Surface area of the exhibition rooms: 860 m.

- Surface area of the Giacometti Courtyard: 450 m.

- Number of visitors since the Foundation's opening: (5,380,000 including 109,690 for the Malraux exhibition in 1973, 119,000 for the Chagall exhibition in 1984 and 146,400 for *L'Œuvre Ultime* in 1989.

- Number of exhibitions held at the Foundation: 105 from April 1966 to November 2003.

- Number of catalogues published by the Foundation: 98.

- Number of unique works belonging to the Foundation: more than 1,500, including 150 sculptures and 70 drawings by Miró, and 35 sculptures by Giacometti.

- Number of engravings belonging to the Foundation: 6,500.

- Number of volumes in the library: 16,000.

- Number of musical creations: more than a hundred.

- Number of members of the Board of Directors: 11, comprising 8 voluntary members designated by the founders and 3 representatives from the Ministries concerned (Interior and Culture).

- Number of members of the Société des Amis de la Fondation Maeght: 2,500 in 2002.

204

# The Friends of the Maeght Foundation Society

The Société des Amis de la Fondation Maeght, a non-profit making organisation (called Association Loi 1901 after the law of that year relating to associations), has 2,500 members who can take advantage of the many activities proposed: conferences, cultural visits, guided tours of each exhibition, as well as reductions (on Foundation Maeght publications) in the bookshop, loans from the library, posters and catalogues sent by post.

Active Member: 55 € - Couple: 80 € - Student: 25 €
Supporting Member: 125 € - Life Member: 250 €


Subscriptions should be sent to the Maeght Foundation:
Société des Amis, 06570 Saint-Paul.
Telephone: 04.93.32.81.63 - Fax: 04.93.32.53.22
contact@fondation-maeght.com


# Comité Pierre Reverdy

As a result of the close ties that existed between Pierre Reverdy and Marguerite and Aimé Maeght, Mme Pierre Reverdy, following the exhibition in 1970 devoted to the poet, gave, on 18th June 1974, the freehold of her husband's literary work to the Maeght Foundation. Such generosity is rarely to be found in literary history. The agreement stipulates that a Comité Pierre Reverdy (originally presided by Marguerite Maeght and, today, by François Chapon) be responsible for the ethical, intellectual and material administration of this donation. Thus, it is also responsible for the publication of all his works. Respecting the author's intentions is the principal concern behind all the initiatives undertaken with regard to his work. The Foundation is responsible for collecting all his documents, manuscripts, books and portraits which thus become part of the Foundation's collections.

205

# The Marguerite and Aimé Maeght Foundation Guide Book

Authors: Cati Chambon, Yoyo Maeght.

Photographic research: Colette Robin.
Archives: Fondation Maeght.
Book design: Pierre Simonneau and Andréane Burgat-Ruffin.

## The Maeght Foundation

06570 Saint-Paul
Telephone: 04.93.32.81.63 - Telecopie: 04.93.32.53.22
Open every day including Sundays and public holidays
1st October - 30th June:
10 a.m. to 12.30 p.m. and 2.30 p.m. to 6 p.m.
1st July - 30th September:
10 a.m. to 7 p.m.
Car park - Cafeteria

www.maeght.com

# Contents

PHOTOGRAPHIC CREDITS:

Oscar Bailey, Y. Coatsaliou, Pascal Faligot, Fondation Maeght, Galerie Adrien Maeght,
Claude Gaspari, Claude Germain, Jacques Gomot, Paul Guglielmo, Rolf Hegi, Image Art,
Mariette Lachaud, Aimé Maeght, Marguerite Maeght, Léo Mirkine, Jack Nisberg,
A. Ostier, Photo Serge, Jacques Robert, Michel N'Guyen, Étienne-Bertrand Weill.

Translated from French by Médiane, Paris.

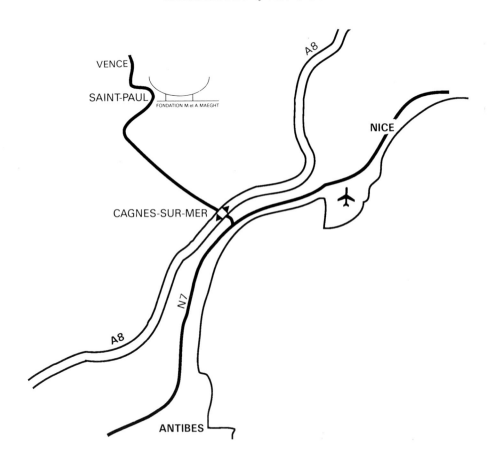

PRINTED BY THE IMPRIMERIE ARTE ADRIEN MAEGHT
ON 20TH JUNE 2003
ISBN ENGLISH: 2-86941-221-5
ISBN FRENCH: 2-86941-115-4
ISBN GERMAN: 2-86941-220-7
ISBN ITALIAN: 2-86941-222-3